VGM Opportunities Series

OPPORTUNITIES IN **PHYSICAL THERAPY CAREERS**

Bernice Krumhansl

Revised by
Kathy Siebel

Foreword by
Margaret M. Kotnik, MA, PT
Consultant
Kent State University

VGM Career Horizons
NTC/Contemporary Publishing Group

Library of Congress Cataloging-in-Publication Data

Krumhansl, Bernice.
    Opportunities in physical therapy careers / Bernice Krumhansl ;
foreword by Margaret M. Kotnik.
        p.   cm. — (VGM opportunities series)
    Previously published: 1987.
    Includes bibliographical references.
    ISBN 0-8442-1804-9 (cloth). — ISBN 0-8442-1805-7 (pbk.)
    1. Physical therapy Vocational guidance.   I. Title.   II. Series.
RM705.K78   1999
615.8'2'023—dc21   99-34065
                                                          CIP

Cover photographs: © PhotoDisc, Inc.

Published by VGM Career Horizons
A division of NTC/Contemporary Publishing Group, Inc.
4255 West Touhy Avenue, Lincolnwood (Chicago), Illinois 60712-1975 U.S.A.
Printed in the United States of America
International Standard Book Number: 0-8442-1804-9 (cloth)
                                       0-8442-1805-7 (paper)
00 01 02 03 04 LB 19 18 17 16 15 14 13 12 11 10 9 8 7 6 5 4 3 2 1

CONTENTS

Physical therapy defined. Is physical therapy the career for you? Qualifications. History of physical therapy in medicine. History of physical therapy as a profession. Caring for the handicapped.

Formal education. High school. College or university. Physical therapist assistant. Physical therapist.

Therapist and patient. Patient evaluation. Exercise programs. The "modalities." The physical therapist as an administrator.

A variety of needs and settings. Pediatrics. Public schools. Industrial clinics. Geriatrics. Private practice. The consultant. Home health care. Institutions for the mentally ill and mentally retarded. Treating the blind. Sports medicine. Foreign assignments. Teaching. Research and writing.

ABOUT THE AUTHOR

Bernice Krumhansl was a physical therapist with approximately five decades of professional experience. She received a Bachelor of Arts degree from Notre Dame College of Ohio, in Cleveland, and a certificate in physical therapy from the Cleveland Clinic Foundation. Her continuing education included short courses in arthritis, cystic fibrosis, orthopedics, neurology, proprioceptive neuromuscular facilitation, lower extremity prostheses, manipulation, cardiac care, burns, personnel management, acutherapy, Yoga, computers in physical therapy, education, muscle energy, and cranio-sacral therapy.

Ms. Krumhansl was also in private practice in Cleveland, Ohio, where she served as assistant professor of physical therapy at the Ohio College of Podiatric Medicine. She obtained earlier clinical experience as a staff physical therapist in the cerebral palsy unit of the Association for the Crippled and Disabled, as the chief physical therapist at St. Alexis Hospital in Cleveland. For thirty-four years, she was Director of Physical Therapy at St. Luke's Hospital in Cleveland, where her responsibilities included both clinical and administrative duties, as well as the supervision of the students from several baccalaureate and associate degree programs. In 1966, she received a Special Rehabilitation Research Fellowship from the Vocational Rehabilitation Administration of the Department of Health, Education and Welfare to serve as a consultant at

Wanless Hospital in western India. During these four months she also served as a consultant at Wanless Wadi Chest Hospital and Richardson Hospital of the Leprosy Mission.

In addition to this book, Ms. Krumhansl published approximately seventy articles on physical therapy, history, travel, and writing techniques; four radio scripts; and three juvenile short stories. She also presented more than two-hundred slide lectures on her medical and personal experiences in Asia to benefit Christian medical missions in India.

This edition was revised by Kathy Siebel, a former career books editor and current resume expert, educator, and writer in the career field.

FOREWORD

Choosing a career is one of the most important and difficult life tasks facing young men and women. There is so much that is unknown and not yet experienced, but decisions must be made, often in haste and without sufficient information. The more information we have, of course, the easier the decision, whether we choose to follow a certain path or take another one leading in another direction.

A book such as *Opportunities in Physical Therapy Careers* is a valuable tool for opening up new areas to the mind for consideration, perusal, meditation. It may lead one on to do more to discover whether one really has the talent or the interest to pursue the field further through volunteer work or through summer employment in an unskilled job in the field, or it may just as firmly convince the reader that the field is definitely not for her or him, which is an equally important decision. In any case, Bernice Krumhansl's book leaves no area unexplored, no fact hidden—it is all there in an engrossing and readable style.

It is not only the reader looking for a vocation who can benefit from this book; it is a revealing study of what physical therapy is all about for the person who is now called "a patient," and is faced with a new problem requiring a form of treatment of which he or she was only vaguely aware before her or his back failed or when arthritis was only a fleeting and vague pain.

The professional or technical student of physical therapy will find new insights and revelations about her or his chosen field as Ms. Krumhansl takes us backward into time to tell us the fascinating facts about the early forms of physical healing or about the evolution of massage and hydrotherapy from their natural and unsophisticated roots to their high-tech image of today.

I have used the earlier edition of this book successfully in my introductory classes in Physical Therapist Assisting at Cuyahoga Community College. Nowhere is there a more lucid description of the history of the profession, the American Physical Therapy Association, or the dynamics of physical therapy today than can be found in *Opportunities in Physical Therapy Careers*. I recommend it with enthusiasm to all who wish to experience this rewarding health career as it is seen through the eyes of one of the country's most creative practitioners of physical therapy.

Margaret M. Kotnik, MA, PT
Consultant
Kent State University
Development of Physical Therapist Assistant Program
On-Site Team Leader
American Physical Therapy Association
Program in Accreditation of Physical Therapist
    Assistant Programs

ACKNOWLEDGMENTS

Eleanor Leuser, Cleveland College faculty of Case Western Reserve University, for her kindly criticism of the manuscript, her encouragement, and her genuine interest in physical therapy and appreciation of its contributions to society.

Sara Rogers and Cora Alice Taylor, formerly in the Division of Education of the American Physical Therapy Association, for recommending me to VGM.

Dr. Marilyn Moffitt, current president of the American Physical Therapy Association, and Ms. Phyllis Quin, of the Membership Section.

Elizabeth Davis, Elizabeth Fellows, and other former members of the national office of the American Physical Therapy Association, for the material they provided for this book.

The directors of programs for physical therapist assistants, for the information they provided in the questionnaire.

To Dr. Mary Edmonds Miles, former director of the physical therapy program of Cleveland State University, and currently a vice-president at Stanford University. To Margaret Forker-Kotnik, former director of the physical therapist assistant program at Cuyahoga Community College in Cleveland, Ohio, for supplying instant answers to many questions, and for much printed material.

The professional, subprofessional, and nonprofessional staff of the physical therapy department of St. Luke's Hospital, Cleveland, Ohio, for their consideration, cooperation, and understanding.

The physical therapists at Wilcox Hospital Clinical Services, Lihue, Hawaii, for their assistance with the revision of the book.

Kathy Siebel, Kalaheo, Hawaii, for her assistance with updating and revising the book.

CHAPTER 1

HISTORY AND OVERVIEW OF PHYSICAL THERAPY

What do you want to do with your life? You probably have heard this question dozens of times and probably have changed your mind dozens of times. Perhaps you already know that for every doctor in our complex medical centers there are several "associated health workers" involved in patient care. In earlier days, doctors usually had a one-on-one relationship with their patients, Today, however, doctors delegate the performance of certain tests, measurements, and treatments to other qualified personnel because modern doctors do not have the time to assume responsibility for all phases of patient care. One group of professionals to whom doctors delegate is that of physical therapists.

PHYSICAL THERAPY DEFINED

Literally, *physical therapy* means "treatment with physical agents." In the earlier days of the profession, therapy was described as "the diagnosis and treatment of disabilities and diseases by the use of physical agents."

A new more encompassing definition and description comes from the *Occupational Outlook Handbook*:

> Physical therapists provide services that help restore function, improve mobility, relieve pain, and prevent or limit permanent disabilities of patients suffering from injuries or disease. They restore, maintain and promote overall fitness and health. Their patients include accident victims and individuals with disabling conditions such as low back pain, arthritis, heart disease, fractures, head injuries, and cerebral palsy.

Physical therapy has often been called "the cornerstone of rehabilitation" because the long road back from injury or disease begins with physical therapy treatments to relieve pain and restore function. If the therapist is to give each patient complete and comprehensive care during the long process of rehabilitation, he or she cannot work in a vacuum. A physical therapist must work closely with the physician, occupational therapist, social service worker, speech pathologist, psychologist, orthopedist and prosthetist, and vocational guidance worker.

IS PHYSICAL THERAPY THE CAREER FOR YOU?

Have you considered why you are thinking of becoming a physical therapist? Is it because you, or someone dear to you, recovered more rapidly from an accident or illness after physical therapy relieved pain and restored function?

Are you a high school or college athlete who wishes to use his or her own motor skills and knowledge of coordination and endurance-building activities to help another person walk and become independent again?

Are you a young person who looks forward to the love and security of marriage and a family, but who desires a health career that will challenge your ingenuity without requiring the long years of study necessary to become a physician?

The choice of a career is one of the most important decisions you will have to make. It will influence not only the way you earn your living, but the place where you live and the people you will meet. Because the choice of a career has such long-reaching and all-encompassing effects, the decision must be both emotional and practical.

Emotionally, you must *want* to enter a service profession, and you must enjoy working with people of all intellectual and social levels because your coworkers and your patients will come from all segments of the population. You must not fear or resent touching or being touched because physical therapy requires a great deal of close personal contact.

Practically, you must consider the job potential. Spending many years and many thousands of dollars preparing for a career in an already overpopulated profession is neither sound nor sensible.

Fortunately, the job outlook for physical therapy is excellent. Although some worry about the field becoming overcrowded, the government predicts that physical therapy careers will continue to be among the fastest growing careers.

According to the *Occupational Outlook Handbook,* physical therapists held 115,000 jobs in 1996. That number is expected to grow as the population ages. The baby boom generation is now at greater risk for illnesses like stroke and heart attack, so more of them may eventually need the services of a physical therapist. At the other end of the spectrum, more newborns with severe birth defects are surviving and more young people are surviving traumatic accidents. All these trends suggest that physical therapists will be in greater demand in years to come.

Physical therapists are also being used in a more proactive way—to prevent illness and injury. They may be hired to evaluate the safety of work sites, to teach safe work habits, or to design exercise programs. Many companies invest in the safety and wellness of their employees, and, therefore, they turn to physical therapists for assistance.

QUALIFICATIONS

Because physical therapy involves serving patients with impaired functions, physical therapists strive to improve their own coordination, and their sense of rhythm, movement, and balance. Before the therapist can teach correct posture to patients, he or she must possess and practice correct posture. Physical therapy is hard work; most therapists have strong hands, endurance, stamina, and a high energy level. According to the *Occupational Outlook Handbook,* physical therapy is "physically demanding. Therapists stoop, knead, crouch, and stand for long periods. Physical therapists move heavy equipment and lift patients or help them turn, stand, or walk."

In the earliest years of the profession, most physical therapists were physical education graduates. Although this is no longer a requirement, many still have had a great deal of experience in swimming, dance, or other athletic background.

Physical therapy courses are difficult, and average-to-superior intelligence is required. Also, the field is constantly changing and growing, making continuing self-education necessary. As in all fields, computer literacy is an advantage both in getting through school and in staying up-to-date after entering the work force.

Scientific aptitude is essential. Several science courses are included in the prerequisites for the physical therapy courses, and students have to read a great deal of scientific literature. Remember that physical therapy curricula require a minimum grade point average ranging from 2.5 to 3.5 (out of 4.0), depending upon the university where the work is done.

Perhaps the most important quality a physical therapist must possess is emotional stability. Because the therapist's life is usually busy to the point of being hectic, and decision making is a constant and ongoing responsibility, he or she must be able to think quickly. There is little or no time for meditation.

Most physical therapists deal constantly with patients who are ill, so some stressful situations may occur. But patients who receive physical therapy are getting better, so they usually are optimistic and obey directions eagerly. A few, however, have terminal illnesses. It is necessary to sympathize and empathize with these patients. However, sometimes the best thing for the patient may be prodding and insistence upon independence.

Occasionally, a patient in a general hospital or nursing home may develop cardiac or pulmonary arrest—the stoppage of the heartbeat or breathing. A few patients have died in physical therapy departments, and more will die there in the years to come because physical therapists are treating more very old, very ill people. The death of a patient during treatment can be an extremely disturbing experience.

Day-to-day care of patients usually is less traumatic, but it certainly has its disagreeable aspects—especially for student therapists and those who are new to the profession. Physical therapists treat patients who have been badly burned, who have deep and odorous ulcers, or who cough and spit up lung secretions. Patients are people who are sick, and they don't stop being sick during their physical therapy sessions. Occasionally, patients will vomit or have bowel or bladder movements during treatment. Then it is necessary for the therapist to wash the patient and clean the floor.

Tact is an important personality trait for the physical therapist to possess, because people are your business. You won't be working just with machinery or laboratory equipment. Patients are living individuals who, when you encounter them, will be in physical and emotional crises. You must be able to inspire confidence in them and build a solid working framework with them and their families.

Moderate mechanical aptitude is helpful, too. Knowing how to handle a screwdriver, a hammer, and a wrench is useful. It isn't necessary to understand all the intricate workings of the machines you use, but you will have to be able to lengthen and shorten crutches and canes. Mechanical ingenuity, the ability to conceive and develop new devices, is a great asset because many physical therapists are called upon to improve and adapt self-help equipment.

Some knowledge of the fundamentals of basic office procedures is also important, particularly the principles of budgeting and accounting.

Dealing with people demands a good vocabulary and the ability to speak and write clearly, You will be directing patients, teaching families, instructing nursing school classes, supervising physical therapy students, reporting on patients' progress to doctors, and demonstrating physical therapy procedures at medical staff conferences. You must be able to write effectively because you will be preparing clinical notes on your patients, annual reports of the department's activities to the hospital board of trustees, and letters to business leaders and prospective employers.

People come in all sizes, shapes, colors, religions, ethnic backgrounds, social levels, and tax brackets. If you cannot deal with people as they are, with love, understanding, and total acceptance, physical therapy is not the career for you. Because duties, especially those in the clinical field, involve very close contact with patients, it is necessary that you be willing to have close bodily contact with people, no matter how beautiful or ugly, brilliant or stupid, rich or poor they are. You must also be able to shift your mental gears very quickly because you must adapt to different personalities in rapid succession.

Most physical therapists are of above-average intelligence and are happy, boisterous, athletic, and optimistic people. No rule states that a physical therapist may not be introverted, but because the profession's responsibilities involve people as patients, people as coworkers, and people on the hospital or agency staff, the gregarious individual may find the field more appealing and easier to work in.

As a physical therapist, you must be innovative, looking constantly for improved methods of performance. You must be analytical in order to compare the patient's performance from one day to the next, to compare patients with the same problems, and to determine how new approaches to old problems can be tried.

You will need to be courageous. Sometimes it takes courage to convince a physician that a different approach to treatment is worth trying. It will take even more courage to fight a legislative assembly in the state capital, or in Washington, for the rights you think are legally yours.

Many people believe the pioneer era in our national history has ended. But pioneering still exists, not on the western frontier, but on the frontiers of science. Pioneers on any frontier must possess the same basic characteristics. First, they must be nonconformists, willing to take criticism for what they believe in. They must have the physical ability to work long hours, sometimes against overwhelming odds, to achieve their goals. They must thrive on the adventure of new ideas and opportunities.

Robert Service, in his ballad "The Land of Beyond," describes the pioneer's personality and attitudes:

> Thank God! there is always a Land of Beyond
> For us who are true to the trail;
> A vision to seek, a beckoning peak,
> A fairness that never will fail;
> A pride in our soul that mocks at a goal,
> A manhood that irks at a bond,
> And try how we will, unattainable still
> Behold it, our Land of Beyond*

Is physical therapy your Land of Beyond?

---

*From *The Collected Poems of Robert Service,* published by Dodd, Mead and Co. Reprinted by permission of the publisher.

HISTORY OF PHYSICAL THERAPY IN MEDICINE

Physical therapy is probably the oldest method of medical treatment. When a caveman hurt his back lifting a rock, he probably lay on hot sand to relieve the pain. When his arthritic joints ached (we know he had arthritis), he probably applied the rocks heating beside his cooking fire because he had observed that stone retained heat for long periods. When he scraped his arm on brush or rocks and it became infected, he probably bathed his wounds in running streams. When he stumbled over a fallen tree trunk, he rubbed (massaged) his shin. He knew the importance of physical fitness because if he lost his endurance, speed, or sure-footedness, he lost his race with the next predator he met—and perhaps his life. He observed that when the sun shone brightly for long hours in the summer, his wounds healed faster than they did in the short, gray days of winter.

The Use of Heat and Cold

Thousands of years later, the Egyptians worshipped the sun's healing powers and erected temples to the sun god Ra. The Greeks worshipped Phoebus Apollo as a sun god. In India the Aryans idolized Savitar as a sun god and divine physician, and in Persia, Mithra was the god of sun and healing. In Germany, Wotan-Odin was the god of healing, and people called the sun Wotan's Eye; they also had Odin's fields, recovery places in the sunlight where the sick went to recuperate. In Peru, the pre-Incans and Incans used the sun to heat their houses and water, and to improve their health. People seem to use heat intuitively. It is effective, generally available in some form, and relatively inexpensive and safe.

The Greeks were the first to use fever therapy as treatment. The Romans were the first to claim relief of pain from the use of hot wax. Many Roman patients lay on heated sheep hides, rolling from side to side. Their methods would seem primitive and strange today, of course, but many of the principles are still sound.

The Renaissance in Europe sparked the reawakening of art and literature, but it was the Industrial Revolution that revived crafts, commerce, and business. When bakeries arose in France, many doctors ordered "stoving" for arthritic patients. The patient was lifted into a hot oven after the bread has been taken out. A few years back, physical therapists placed patients in fever cabinets—essentially the same thing.

A popular treatment in more recent years has been cryotherapy, or the use of ice or cold. Although Roman emperors used snow to cool water and wine, and a few Persian caliphs and emirs enjoyed sherbets, the use of ice was never widespread because it could not be produced artificially until 1750. A few early Greek and Roman physicians recommended cold drinks to combat fever. Early Russians used ice more extensively because it was plentiful. They used ice packs to reduce high fevers, to control infections, and to treat wounds and meningitis. They also used it long ago for treatment of diseases of the central nervous system, an application that is relatively new in the United States. Arthritic Russians and those suffering from gout responded well to ice in the 1800s, but only recently has this treatment for arthritis been introduced to America. Napoleon's surgeons observed in their Russian campaign that amputations of frozen legs were easier, less bloody, and generally more successful than other methods. A revolutionary use of ice in America came from the Vallejo Rehabilitation Center in California, where patients with multiple sclerosis are plunged into a tub of thirty-four-degree ice water for four minutes.

Hypertherapy, or heat in the form of microtherm or ultra-sound treatment, has been used in experimental cancer research and treatment.

Hydrotherapy

The use of water for healing began when primitive people bathed their wounds in running streams. Later, the religions of more civilized cultures endowed water with sacred healing properties. The Hindus believed that the Ganges River and six other sacred waters had healing power. Egyptians conferred the same status on the Nile. The Greeks made frequent use of baths in treating wounds, and we read in Homer that the wounded Hector was cured in this way. Galen used water to treat his wounded and injured athletes. Many Native American tribes used sweatbaths and other rituals involving water therapies, some of which are still in use today.

The Romans were the first people we know of who made extensive use of hydrotherapy. They had eight hundred public baths at one time, charging adults a small fee and admitting children free. They had "sweat houses" with hot and cold rooms— the forerunners of the modern Turkish bath. The Romans were also the first to use underwater exercises in warm springs to treat paralysis from war wounds, as well as the pains of normal aging in the civilian population.

In modern times, the spas of Europe have become famous health resorts, and the hot springs in many parts of the United States are treatment centers. The Scandinavians, especially the Finns, have used sauna baths extensively, and this, too, has become a popular treatment in the United States.

The first documented use of hydrotherapy in military medicine was in the French Revolution, when a surgeon reported his success in treating wounds with large quantities of hot water.

At approximately the same time, an Austrian peasant, injured by a fall from a horse, treated himself with hot packs similar to those he used on his animals. His cure was so spectacular that he became famous and began teaching foreign physicians his method. Today we use Hydrocollator packs to relieve pain and heal the sick.

Electrotherapy

The use of electricity for therapy originated in 641 B.C. when Thales of Miletus discovered that amber, when rubbed vigorously, attracted light objects to itself. Also in ancient times, a number of people claimed healing properties from contact with electric "eels," electric catfish, and other fish known to give off electric shocks. (This electrical property of some fish species is presumed to be a method of self-defense, so any healing properties would be one of nature's strange accidents.) Eventually, a Roman official suggested the deliberate application of electric fish to gain the benefits of the shock. In A.D. 400, a Greek physician suggested holding a magnet over the arthritic joints of his patients.

Until approximately 1600 no real advances were made in the use of electricity in medicine. The British scientists William Gilbert and Gilbert Colchester began research on electrotherapy, and Dr. Colchester published a treatise titled "de Magnete." At about the same time, John Wesley wrote the first book in English on electrotherapy.

Each generation and each nation since then has contributed to the development of electrotherapy, but the great heroes are Luigi Galvani, Michael Faraday, and Alessandro Volta.

When electricity became a part of everyday living, life changed dramatically, and so did medicine. Scientists were able to produce heat and cold and to regulate temperatures. In 1934, a scientist developed a form of heat using high-frequency current. This was called *long-wave diathermy.* It was subsequently improved to *short-wave diathermy* for more effective treatment and easier application. This is the same form of heat as the inductotherm used in steel mills. More recently, Dr. Frank Krusen, a physiatrist at the Mayo Clinic, produced another method of using extremely short waves, which he called *microwave* or *microtherm.*

On the eve of World War II, German scientists were working on adapting sound waves for use as a therapeutic agent. The war interrupted the program, but, in 1949, reports on the results of research projects on sound were made by seventy-five scientists. By the mid-1950s, *ultrasound* was an important treatment modality.

Massage and Exercise

An ancient, and unfortunately anonymous, medical historian wrote, "Nature early taught man to knead his flesh and bend his body to relieve him of certain ills." Although some cultures regarded massage and exercise as separate forms of treatment, most areas of the world used the massage and exercise combination.

In 3000 B.C., Kong-Fu, a Chinese practitioner, wrote a book on the value of massage and exercise. The Japanese also used massage extensively during the same period. The Hindus, too, were among the first to use therapeutic exercises. In the Vedic legends, which are the origin of the Hindu religion, there are detailed descriptions of postural exercises to cure specific diseases. Today in India, Ayurvedic physicians still rely on the Yoga positions to cure physical and mental illness.

Ancient Greek gymnasts were teachers of massage and exercise. They directed the treatment of fractures, dislocations, and other traumatic injuries. Greek physicians gained much of their knowledge from gymnasts. Galen (A.D. 130–201), who gave the first accurate description of bones and muscles, was the surgeon of the Roman gladiators. There are frequent references in the Bible and in Greek and Roman poetry to "anointing with oils," undoubtedly a form of massage.

During the Dark and Middle Ages of Europe, medicine was kept alive in the Western World in the Arab-dominated areas. Several Islamic physicians refer to the use of massage and exercise. In the thirteenth century, two Middle Eastern authors reported on the hygienic and therapeutic effects of exercise. In the sixteenth century, there were three major works on the value of physical agents, massage, and exercise in the treatment of diseases and injuries. By the seventeenth century, two of England's famous surgeons were writing about the value of exercise, and by the middle of the eighteenth century, French and German physicians were writing of the effect of massage on circulation and general health.

The story of therapeutic exercises in modern times is tied closely to the life of Sweden's Pehr Henri Ling (1776–1839). Ling studied theology and had a brief career in the navy before, in 1805, he received an appointment as Master of Fencing at the University of Lund. Here he developed and taught a new system of movement much different from that of the ancient Greeks, which was then still popular in Sweden. Ling studied anatomy, physiology, and natural sciences. Then he demonstrated that properly employed exercise could remedy disease and bodily defects. In 1813, he established the Central Institute of Massage and Corrective Exercises in Stockholm, the first of many institutes for medical and orthopedic gymnastics throughout Europe and the United States. Resistive exercises originated with the Swedish system, as did isometric exercises.

In 1889, a Swiss physician, H. S. Frenkel, made a great impact on the medical profession when he introduced a series of exercises for patients with certain diseases that affected the nerves and balance centers. Frenkel was the first person to use exercises for the purpose of coordination.

The Chinese have used acupuncture for many centuries to treat a variety of diseases and as an anesthetic. A needle is inserted into sensitive points in the fourteen meridians, or vertical lines, in the body. Later, the Japanese applied pressure to the same points, and called their method "Shiatsu." Today, physical therapists are using acupressure and electrical stimulation on the same ancient Chinese acupoints.

Now, physical therapists are making their own history through research. In clinical practice as well as in research centers, physical therapists are finding out why certain things work and are documenting their own results.

HISTORY OF PHYSICAL THERAPY AS A PROFESSION

As therapeutic medicine developed into a more sophisticated profession, various specialties were formed in order to concentrate on conquering specific diseases.

One group, called *orthopedists,* treated patients who had problems with bones, joints, and muscles. The orthopedists knew the value of heat to relieve pain, of massage to relax muscle spasm, and of exercises to strengthen weak muscles and stretch tight joints and muscles. The application of the combination of heat, massage, and exercise proved too time-consuming for many orthopedists with busy practices. In England, toward the end of the nineteenth century, British orthopedists selected young women who were graduates of schools of physical education to administer these special treatments. Because of their physical education background, they had a knowledge of anatomy, physiology, and kinesiology (muscle function). The orthopedists trained them on the job, as apprentices, to direct the special corrective exercises of orthopedic patients.

On the opposite side of the Atlantic, from 1915 to 1917, a polio epidemic swept the United States. Dr. Robert Lovett of Vermont copied the British example and trained two women, Wilhelmine Wright and Janet Merrill, in the muscular re-education techniques for the treatment of poliomyelitis or, as it was then called, infantile paralysis.

In 1917, the United States entered World War I. Battle casualties most frequently involved orthopedic injuries of arms and legs. Because physical training and muscle re-education were not a part of nursing, medical, or surgical care, the Surgeon General's office formed a new department. It was called the Women's Auxiliary Aides, under the Division of Orthopedic Surgery, and it assumed responsibility for this phase of caring for the wounded.

In 1916, the first American physical therapy department was established at Walter Reed Hospital, in Washington, DC. It consisted of two small rooms in the basement. This undoubtedly established a fashion in physical therapy departments, because for years departments continued to be tucked away in hospital basements. That first department at Walter Reed Hospital was so small that most of the treatments had to be given at the patient's bedside.

When World War I began, there were no established schools of physical therapy in the United States. The only qualified person in the Army was Marguerite Sanderson, who quickly organized a crash course in physical therapy at Walter Reed Hospital.

As soon as the battle casualties began arriving, it was obvious that the Army would need more therapists than one school could produce. Soon, fourteen more schools opened in different parts of the country. Their graduates received a new title: *Reconstruction Aide.*

An outstanding leader in the development of physical therapy education in this country, and one who was generally instrumental in fostering the progress of physical therapy as a profession, was Mary McMillan. During World War I she directed the training of reconstruction aides at Reed College in Eugene, Oregon. This college produced the largest number of graduates during the war.

During the two war years, fourteen schools trained eight hundred physical education teachers to become reconstruction aides, and three hundred of them served overseas. At the beginning of the war they served with the Army as civilians. Although they had to obey all the military rules, they did not receive any of the military benefits. Byron's line "Among them, not of them" seems to describe their plight.

When the war ended, civilian practice wasn't ready for the specialty of physical therapy. The reconstruction aides returned to the teaching of physical education, or other occupations.

A few schools continued teaching physical therapy. Dr. Frank Granger, a staunch advocate of physical therapy, and Mary McMillan codirected a course of study at the Harvard Medical School. This course emphasized electrophysics, electrotherapy, and muscle re-education.

When the country had adjusted to civilian life, a few of the reconstruction aides met for dinner at Keene's Chop House in New York City, on January 15, 1921, to form an organization that they called the American Women's Physical Therapeutic Association. Its 245 members elected Mary McMillan as their president.

A year later, when they decided to include men in the group, they changed the name to the American Physiotherapy Association. In March 1921, they began publishing a quarterly journal to inform members of the newest advances in physical therapy. By 1928, the *Physical Therapy Review* was being published bimonthly, and in 1931, after the first decade of its existence, the organization had 534 members.

The American Medical Association in 1925 established a Council on Physical Therapy. They outlined courses to be given in medical schools. Graduate nurses and graduates from schools of physical education were accepted for a nine-month course. By 1940, there were sixteen schools graduating 135 students a year. One school had begun to offer a bachelor's degree course. The field of physical therapy was gaining momentum. There were approximately one thousand active therapists and two hundred inactive therapists in the United States.

The entrance of the United States into World War II created an urgent need for a greater number of therapists than the existing schools could possibly supply. To meet this need, seven army hospitals and several private hospitals instituted courses, and fifteen civilian schools accelerated their courses.

To avert some of the problems of World War I, Congress declared in December 1942, that a qualified physical therapist would receive the rank of second lieutenant in the Army. Women holding a bachelor's degree who had graduated from approved schools of physical therapy were eligible for a commission in the Women Appointed for

Voluntary Emergency Service (WAVES). The WAVES did not receive foreign assignments. During the war, sixteen hundred women served in the Army and eight hundred went overseas—about half to the European-Mediterranean theater and the other half to the Pacific.

The war record of physical therapists is inspiring. The Japanese captured and imprisoned several physical therapists. One of these was Mary McMillan. When the Japanese bombed Pearl Harbor, she was in Manila waiting for a ship to take her back to her teaching post at the Medical College in Peking. She went to the Army hospital immediately, and volunteered to serve for the duration of the war as a physical therapist. Her second Army stretch lasted only a few days. She spent all the war years in the prison camp of Santo Tomas, trying to aid and comfort other prisoners. Another physical therapist serving in southeast Asia received an award for her espionage work in Indonesia. When the war ended, most of the schools discontinued the short emergency courses but, by 1946, twenty-one schools had a capacity for 480 students.

In 1944, the United States suffered the worst polio epidemic in history, with 14,500 cited cases. In 1945, the National Foundation for Infantile Paralysis gave the American Physiotherapy Association $1,267,000 for two thousand scholarships to train physical therapists and other necessary personnel. Simultaneously, the therapists at Warm Springs, Georgia, were developing many new treatment procedures for polio. Many of these were applicable to other disease and mechanical problems, also.

The 1940s were important years for physical therapy. Battlefront casualties, industrial accidents in defense plants, and polio epidemics brought the attention of the public to the necessity for physical therapy. Physical therapy was no longer a pioneer field. In the 1950s several baccalaureate programs were developing, and graduate school courses were being planned.

As the number of physical therapists increased, the strength of the American Physical Therapy Association grew. There are now fifty-seven chapters in the fifty states, Washington, DC, and Puerto Rico. *The Journal of the American Physical Therapy Association* has received an award for excellence in its category. In 1971, the APTA celebrated its fiftieth anniversary in Boston, looking back to its years of challenge and rejoicing in its achievements. The succeeding years brought even more exciting periods of development and change.

Today we stand on the brink of new research. Biomechanical engineers are devising new types of braces and artificial limbs. Physiatrists are developing many new kinds of equipment that represent dramatic improvements to relieve pain. Several research centers are working on programs using computerized equipment to enable paralyzed patients to become partially independent. New information on muscle function and neurology has increased the efficacy of rehabilitation programs in many areas.

CARING FOR THE HANDICAPPED

During the past half century there has been a growing understanding and acceptance of the handicapped person as "a person with a handicap." Everyone, whatever his or her physical abilities and challenges, is a person with the same basic sensitivity, emotions, desires, and drives. Although total independence is the patient's goal, the damage caused by a disease or injury may be irreparable. In such a case, the rehabilitation plan must teach the patient to live with the disability.

The word *disability* is not synonymous with the words *disease, injury,* or *defect.* Physical therapists often use the word disability to describe the conditions of patients that, in some way, make them physically handicapped. Such conditions frequently prevent the patients from functioning independently and can make them physically, emotionally, and financially dependent on others. While diseases, injuries, or physical defects may cause disabilities, the presence of such conditions is not always considered a disability. In addition, disability can result when a condition is inadequately treated or when a condition is mismanaged. The rehabilitation of the disabled is now emerging as a major challenge to modern society, and laws like the Americans with Disabilities Act protect the rights of the disabled. The associated health professions must unite to meet this challenge.

The combination of religious, ethical, and social development in the United States today has resulted in our recognition of the responsibility of caring for disabled citizens by providing them with housing, food, and medical care, if they cannot provide these things for themselves. Few private citizens have the financial resources to assume care of another person burdened with large medical bills.

The federal government and every state government provide for medical aid and vocational training for the handicapped. At the national level, the Department of Health has investigated the problems of the handicapped of all ages both in urban and rural communities.

The goal of federal and state programs is to restore handicapped persons' independence. However, funding for these programs varies because it is tied to the federal and state budgets. Therefore, the availability of these services changes from year to year and from one geographic region to another. As our nation ages and the number of persons who could benefit from physical therapy grows, the federal and state programs will face difficult choices about how to ensure quality care and how to fund it.

Given the cost of physical therapy and the growing demand for services, we must be realistic about patient outcomes. Physical therapists can help by getting to know patients and their families and by helping them set goals. While a full recovery is always the goal, it will never be possible or practical for every patient. Therefore, some patients may decide to work in a sheltered shop where they perform simple repetitive motions in a noncompetitive environment and earn a minimal salary. Some patients learn to manage a house, so that their spouses can maintain paid employment outside the home. Some patients never advance beyond basic activities of eating and personal hygiene, and some remain dependent on complete custodial care in a nursing home.

Rehabilitation is not a magic word. It began with a philosophy, became an objective, and developed into a method of coordinating services of several specialties in the allied health fields. Those who work in rehabilitation have serious responsibilities because they must blend academic scientific knowledge with wisdom born of experience and boldness born of faith.

CHAPTER 2

EDUCATIONAL BACKGROUND AND TRAINING

You will learn a great deal about the history, the philosophy, and the duties involved in physical therapy by reading; but seeing a physical therapist in action in a typical setting will teach you more than all the books can offer.

You can begin by calling your local hospital and making an appointment with the director of the physical therapy department for an interview and a tour of the department. After this first introduction, try to get some work experience in the field. Ask the director of the department if there is an opening available as a vacation replacement aide or orderly. If there is a job, apply for it, but if there is none, contact the director of volunteers to inquire about serving on Saturday mornings or one day a week as a volunteer.

If you land the job, report for work every day, be on time, and don't skip out early when the boss is attending a meeting. Value the job, and show it in your attitude toward the job's requirements.

If you accept a job as a temporary employee, you must work as long as you specified on the application. Don't decide halfway through the summer that a canoe trip is more fun than a job and quit with a day's notice. Leaving will cause a great deal of difficulty for the department; it will be impractical to hire someone for a few weeks, and working short-staffed puts an added strain on all the people you leave. Besides the difficulties you cause, it points out to the director of the department that you lack the maturity and depth for a service career in the health field. The director may never give you another opportunity to work for her or him, nor will that director ever give you a recommendation to work for anyone else, much less a recommendation for enrollment in a physical therapy course.

As an aide or orderly, you will transport patients from their rooms to the physical therapy department in wheelchairs or on carts. You will make up treatment tables with fresh linen, empty laundry hampers and sort fresh linen, clean hydrotherapy equipment, and occasionally clean other machines. You may help with clerical work. You will have an opportunity to help the therapists "transfer" patients—that is, move them from one place to another, but there will be little more you will be able to do in direct patient care. The therapists in the department will know you are interested in the field as a possible career, and they will invite you to watch interesting procedures when the work schedule allows it. You will be able to see the chain of command in a department, you will learn to talk with patients, and you will become familiar with the types of disabilities that physical therapists handle.

You may prefer to work outdoors as a counselor in a summer camp for handicapped children. Spending a summer as a camp counselor can be a rich and rewarding experience as well as fun. It is, however, not a typical physical therapy situation. A better investment of your time would be to spend a summer working in a hospital.

While you are working or volunteering, or just considering a career in physical therapy, it would be beneficial to read several books about the work. One description of the working life of a physical therapist can be found in *Your Career in Physical Therapy* by Patricia and Ray Darby. Patricia Darby is a physical therapist; Ray Darby is a professional writer. Two novels, *Laurie, Physical Therapist* by Lois Habart, and *Janet Moore, Physical Therapist* by Alice Colvert, are also good reading. (There is as yet no known book with a male central character.) Another book that opens the horizons of a foreign work experience is *Erica and the King,* by Erica Leuchtag. This is an account of Ms. Leuchtag's experiences in Nepal, when she rehabilitated the queen and participated in the overthrow of the Rana regime and the reestablishment of the monarchy.

Ask your department director to notify you when the local chapter will be showing several of the recruitment films made by the American Physical Therapy Association.

Physical therapy is a popular career choice, and competition for admission into physical therapy programs is intense. By 2001 all programs for physical therapy will be at the master's degree level and above. To gain admission to these programs, students will need good undergraduate grades and volunteer experience in physical therapy.

FORMAL EDUCATION

Your education for a career in physical therapy must include a balanced combination of courses that will teach you how to live as well as how to earn a living. You must develop an understanding of humanity's spiritual and social needs as well as our physical requirements. You must learn to think logically, to analyze, and to interpret. You must be able to write and speak effectively. You must learn how to establish good interpersonal relationships. After you have built this foundation, you can begin planning for your professional courses. Today's requirements for admission into a physical therapy course are higher than ever before, because scholarship makes the difference between a craft and a profession.

HIGH SCHOOL

Your education should include a college preparatory course in high school. In general, this should consist of four years of English, with both speech and journalism courses, if possible. Take two years of a foreign language, two years of mathematics, and one year each of biology, chemistry, physics, history, social science, first aid, health, business, and computer science.

COLLEGE OR UNIVERSITY

According to the American Physical Therapy Association, 173 physical therapy programs were operating as of July 1997. Forty-six of these offer bachelor's degrees. One hundred and sixteen offer a master's degree in physical therapy. By 2001, according to the *Occupational Outlook Handbook,* all accredited programs will be at the master's degree level and above.

In addition to requiring work in the basic sciences, bachelor's programs now include courses in biomechanics, neuroanatomy, human growth and development, manifestations of disease, exam techniques, and therapeutic procedures. Those who major in a related field may choose to pursue a master's in physical therapy.

A list of programs appears in the appendix to this book.

PHYSICAL THERAPIST ASSISTANT

Because the need and demand for physical therapy increased so rapidly after World War II, in 1967 the American Physical Therapy Association established the Physical Therapist Assistant program. The APTA, which had established the educational requirements for physical therapists, decided upon a two-year associate degree program that gives students both theoretical and practical knowledge, but that stresses the practical application—the *how* rather than the *why*.

If you decide upon this two-year program, the freshman year curriculum will include many liberal arts courses to provide you with a foundation for intellectual, social, and cultural growth. This background differs from that in a vocational or skill-oriented field. Some schools introduce physical therapy in the freshman year, but others do not offer physical therapy courses until the sophomore year. During the latter part of the course you will spend some time in hospitals, nursing homes, and children's centers to apply what you learned in your classes.

Every job and every level of physical therapy has advantages and disadvantages. That of the physical therapist assistant is no exception.

The two-year course is less expensive than the four-year baccalaureate program. If you are hesitant to take on a sizable loan to finance your education, you can begin working in two years, and you continue your education by attending evening courses at a nearby college or university. This would enable you to enroll later in a baccalaureate program.

Many hospitals give employees the fringe benefit of certain professional courses or college credit hours. Also, most universities give free credit hours to members of physical therapy departments where their students are assigned for clinical experience. Depending upon many circumstances, it might be possible for you to receive part of your education free. Remember, these fringe benefits are not routine, nor are they inherent in every job, but they do exist in some places.

One great advantage in working as an assistant is having constant association with patients. Your time is not diverted into administrative details or teaching.

The salary of the assistant varies from $5.15 to $15.00 per hour.

One major disadvantage is that an assistant cannot advance up the professional ladder into the other positions open to the physical therapist with a baccalaureate or master's degree.

Very few junior colleges have open-end programs with universities that would allow a graduate with an associate degree to continue in the junior year in a baccalaureate program.

Usually, associate degree graduates must take several courses to enter the baccalaureate program and then may have to repeat some of the junior college work, depending upon the requirements of the university they enter.

The assistant may not evaluate or assess a patient, nor make judgments pertaining to therapy, except in simple, routine situations. In some states, the assistant may not work unless a therapist is on duty to give direct supervision. In other areas, it is possible for the assistant to treat a patient after the therapist has performed the initial evaluation, even though the therapist may not be present. The latter approach will probably become the custom and the law in a very short time.

The potential of job definitions is very speculative at this time. Some authorities are forecasting that in a very short time physical therapists will be acting as department directors—supervising, evaluating, teaching, and administering—while the assistant will perform all the more routine duties related to direct patient care. Other leaders point out that many hospitals with limited budgets prefer to employ therapists whose broader educational bases qualify them for a wider scope of activity, authority, and responsibility. In 1985, Medicare and Blue Cross began an intensive cost-cutting campaign in hospitals. The lower salary of the physical therapist assistant may increase the job potential for this group of employees.

A physical therapist can perform all the treatments that an assistant can perform, but an assistant cannot perform all the treatments that a physical therapist can give.

The role of the assistant is neither subservient nor demeaning. The assistant offers an extension to the arms of the therapist to ensure that all patients' needs will be met as often as they arise.

In the next chapter, you will read the details of all the physical therapy treatment procedures. Those treatments that the assistant gives are whirlpool and Hubbard tank therapy, diathermy, infrared, paraffin, ultraviolet, Jobst intermittent pressure, ultrasound, massage, cervical and lumbar traction, training in exercises and ambulation, teaching Activities of Daily Living, and assisting the physical therapist in some of the more complicated treatments. If you become an assistant, you will have the opportunity to instruct patients in situations where the information is standardized. You will treat patients when rapid or unexpected adjustments are unlikely and where certain vital signs are readily identifiable and easily interpreted. This level of the profession requires some decision making and use of judgment, but does not deal with crucial or demanding situations.

Is this the role for you?

PHYSICAL THERAPIST

Most of the people working in the field today are physical therapists with baccalaureate degrees. Today's students must eventually earn a master's degree, but they begin as physical therapists always have: with the general liberal arts courses required during the first two years of most undergraduate degrees. Liberal arts courses include English composition and literature, a foreign language, philosophy, psychology, speech, history, sociology, anthropology, biology, zoology, bacteriology, embryology, chemistry, physics, and mathematics. Be certain that your general courses include the prerequisites for admission to the physical therapy curriculum. During the final two years, you will be taking courses in professional education.

Physical therapy courses will include human anatomy with cadaver dissection, physiology, biophysics, physics, kinesiology, abnormal psychology, child development, medical lectures in many of the specialties, physical therapy procedures, and professional ethics. While you are in college, take all the physical education courses you can in folk dancing, modern dance, and aerobics. Corrective exercise courses and gymnastics, swimming, and life saving are also helpful.

If you may choose electives, enroll in courses in educational psychology and methods, because you will be teaching people of all levels of education achievement throughout your professional life. You may also be teaching in formal classroom situations. Other electives that might be helpful are public speaking, journalism or business English, behavioral science, organizational behavior, administration, interpersonal behavior, and labor relations. If your computer skills need work, develop them now. Computer science is becoming increasingly important also because computers are used for billing, statistics, and for recording patient progress.

Both physical therapy and physical therapy assistant programs include clinical experience. This begins with a half day per week observation, and expands to working full time, in the final quarter or semester. Students work under the supervision of a therapist. They apply what they have learned in the academic courses. The clinical rotations include acute hospitals, rehabilitation centers, pediatric and geriatric centers, private practice offices, and homebound work.

Some programs assign students to institutions close to the home university. Others, because of their location, or the large number of students, must arrange for clinical facilities farther away. Some programs are very strict about the placement of students, while others are more fluid and will attempt to arrange an affiliation in the student's hometown, even though this may not be one of the usual clinical facilities.

Lodging is provided by most hospitals, usually without charge, to the students, although some may charge a nominal fee. Some give the students free meals, but most do not. Some provide laundry or other personal services. A few give the students a stipend, but this is rare and is becoming rarer with spiraling inflation and increasing governmental surveillance of hospital finances.

Colleges and universities charge a credit hour fee for the period of clinical experience, and the students must pay their own transportation from the school to each of two or three facilities and back to the university for graduation. In considering the total cost of your education, you must plan for these necessary and inevitable expenses during your senior year. You will also need two or three uniforms and duty shoes. Good quality uniforms are rather expensive, but they hold their shape longer and are usually more durable. Some schools have their own uniforms.

In choosing the school for your professional training, you must consider several facts. In most state university programs, competition for seats in the program is very keen. Many of those turned down are qualified applicants. Some state universities accept only students who have had their freshman and sophomore years at that institution, but they may accept one or two transfer students. If the state university in your state does not accept you into the program, it would be wiser, easier, and probably no more expensive to enroll in a private college than to attempt to enroll in a state university in another state, where competition is great and your chances for acceptance are greatly diminished. Rates for nonresident students are usually high. Universities offering programs are listed in the appendix at the back of the book.

There are many advantages for the physical therapist who has a master's degree. When you have had adequate experience, your opportunities for advancement from staff therapist to responsible and interesting positions are numerous. You may be appointed physical therapy educational supervisor in your institution. In this position, you would supervise the clinical students in your institution. You would also arrange and conduct all the in-service programs. You might teach classes of students in the school of nursing or classes of patients. You might even teach interns and residents. You would have the opportunity to advance to the position of assistant director of the department. After this experience, you would be qualified to become the director of a small department, and, later, you would be qualified to assume responsibility for a large department. An increasing number of physical therapists are taking on supervisory roles.

Even as a staff therapist, you would have the authority to evaluate and assess patients. (Physical therapists may not diagnose, so we never use the word "examine"; instead, we use the words "evaluate" or "assess.") After the evaluation, you would plan the treatment program. You should also consider that as a therapist you would treat patients whose medical problems are more interesting than are those assigned to the assistant. Also, the treatment program is more challenging to your initiative and ingenuity.

The same or greater possibilities for tuition assistance exist for therapists as those that were previously described for the assistant.

Recent salary surveys conducted by the American Physical Therapy Association suggest that earnings also vary according to work setting. Physical therapists working in home health and long-term care report the highest earnings; both groups average $60,000. Those employed in clinics earn slightly less, with average annual income of $56,000. In hospitals physical therapists have salaries of $46,500, and in schools they earn $43,500.

The same survey reported that earnings for physical therapy assistants varied similarly according to setting. Physical therapy assistants in home health reported salaries of $38,000. In long-term care they earned $36,000. PTAs working in clinics averaged $32,000 per year, while those in hospitals averaged $30,500. The lowest annual salaries, $28,500 on average, were reported by physical therapy assistants working in school settings.

Federal statistics for 1996 were reported in the *Occupational Outlook Handbook.* They indicate weekly salaries for physical therapists. For 1996, those median salaries were $757 per week. Therapists in the top 10 percent of earnings had weekly income of $1,294. The middle 50 percent had median earnings of $577 to $1,055. The bottom 10 percent reported median income of less than $400 per week.

CHAPTER 3

THE WORK PHYSICAL
THERAPISTS DO

In the previous chapters, you read about the growing need for physical therapists in the health field, and you read what the physical therapist assistant and the physical therapist do, but you didn't read *how* they do these things, and perhaps you wondered how all these things fit together to make a typical working day.

In the most common sequence today, after the patient is referred to physical therapy, a physical therapist will perform an "evaluation." The evaluation procedures are described later in the chapter. All patients treated by physical therapist assistants must first be evaluated by a physical therapist, and the therapist will perform interim evaluations during the course of the treatment series, and perhaps change the treatment plan, as needed.

The patient's progress is documented in clinical notes, which are written at specified intervals, determined by the hospital or the department policy.

Frequently, a therapist will instruct the patient's family in certain procedures to hasten recovery and to prevent deformities or further disability, especially in muscles and joints.

Obviously, the director and the assistant director supervise the work of all the other staff members. In some facilities, the director's responsibilities are purely administrative, with no direct patient care. In others, he or she may be treating patients almost eight hours a day, and performing the administrative details after the department closes. In one extreme instance of this, a director was expected to work sixty hours a week, for forty hours salary.

As you read this, you will realize that direct patient service and departmental administration overlap. However, to show both aspects of the professional obligations more clearly and completely, they have been separated in the explanations that follow.

THERAPIST AND PATIENT

Some physicians will write "Evaluate and Treat" orders, allowing the physical therapist to choose the type of treatment most appropriate for the patient's problem. Other doctors will write very specific treatment orders, including the number of treatments. In most states not requiring a physician's order, the therapist must have the patient's diagnosis from a physician.

As soon as the therapist receives the requisition, he or she learns everything possible about the patient's medical history. If the therapist is not familiar with the diagnosis, he or she will review textbooks for a better understanding of the patient's problems.

If the patient is hospitalized, the therapist must decide whether it is better to administer treatment in the physical therapy department or at bedside. Usually, the only patients who receive treatments at the bedside are those who cannot be moved safely from their beds. Whenever possible, therapists bring their patients to the department because the facilities there are better, they can spend more time with the patients, the change of scenery is stimulating for the patients, and the other patients present offer a great deal of encouragement.

Aides and orderlies transfer patients from beds to carts or wheelchairs, and then transport the patients to the department. They also assist the patients in getting onto the treatment tables and in preparing them for the treatments.

Before a therapist begins any test or treatment, the patient's confidence must be won. This is a simple matter with intelligent and cooperative adults, but much more difficult with frightened children. In handling children, it is often necessary to spend as much time in the emotional preparation for treatment as in the actual treatment.

PATIENT EVALUATION

After establishing a working friendship, the therapist is ready to evaluate the patient. This may be a complex and time-consuming procedure ordered by a doctor to help in the diagnosis of a baffling problem. More frequently, it is a relatively simple assessment of the patient's abilities and limitations.

Types of Diagnostic Tests

Physical therapists perform four types of diagnostic tests: electrical muscle testing, test of voluntary muscle power, joint measurement, and functional activity tests.

The physical therapist may perform tests with electrical currents to determine whether the damage is in the brain, the spinal cord, the nerves carrying the impulse from the spinal cord to the muscle, or in the muscle itself, if a patient has had an injury that causes paralysis or if the patient develops paralysis without any apparent reason.

Where physical therapists once relied on x-rays to gather information, they can now use computed tomography to get a better image of a patient's body. Computed tomography is used in many situations. For example, it helps diagnose and treat patients with spinal stenosis—pain in the lower extremities caused by degenerative diseases that affect the joints.

One test for muscle function is the *electromyographic test.* A doctor or a specially trained therapist inserts a needle into a muscle. When the muscle contracts, it sends out electrical impulses that travel from the muscle through the needle and wires to a writing apparatus attached to a revolving drum. The writing arm records the pattern of the electrical output on a graph. The doctor reads the graph and learns a great deal about the condition of the muscle from the pattern of the electrical waves shown on it.

In another group of electrical tests, the therapist places an active electrode fastened to a pencil-like applicator on the myoneural junction or motor point, the place where the nerve enters the muscle. By observing whether the muscle responds, how it responds, and the amount of time necessary for the contraction, the therapist can determine whether there is damage to the brain, to the peripheral nerve trunks, or to the muscles. After repeated tests, the therapist knows whether a nerve is healing or dying. This description is, of course, an oversimplification of a difficult and time-consuming procedure.

The most common test of a patient's ability to move is the *manual muscle test,* or the test of voluntary muscle power. Manual muscle testing requires patience, practice, and experience, as well as a thorough knowledge of muscle function and substitute motions. In this test, when the patient attempts to perform a certain movement, the therapist observes whether the muscle can take normal resistance to the motion, move the part against gravity, move the part with gravity eliminated, or contract the muscle only without producing any movement. The patient repeats the motion several times so that the therapist can observe the endurance of the muscles.

Muscles can contract strongly and permanently in cases of damage to certain areas of the brain or spinal cord. If a muscle is not able to relax when the opposite muscle contracts, the condition is called *spasticity.* In testing for a spastic muscle, the therapist moves the muscle through the motion to observe whether the muscle jerks, remains contracted, or relaxes.

Muscle testing in the legs usually includes gait analysis. By observing alignment of a patient's bones, in standing and walking, a therapist can confirm findings in other tests for weakness and spasticity. The position of the weak and spastic muscles, the areas of weight bearing in the feet, and the manner in which a patient walks all combine to help the doctor and the therapist decide whether a patient needs braces, lifts, or specific exercises.

Testing procedures are not limited to specific muscles. Many patients receiving physical therapy suffer from brain damage at birth or in old age. These people may have lost their ability to move, their sensation, or their sense of position. Some may have lost part of their vision, while others lose their hearing, and a few lose both. Many older adults who are paralyzed on the side of the dominant hand lose their speech or their understanding of words. Before therapists can begin a program to restore function in the affected arm and leg, they must know the extent of the brain damage. They learn this by observing the patient's performance.

Goniometry is the measurement of joint motion. This is another important part of the testing procedure. The therapist uses a goniometer, an adaptation of the common protractor, to measure how many degrees a joint moves. The therapist repeats the measurement at regular intervals, to gauge how rapidly the patient is recovering function—or possibly to conclude that the patient won't recover any motion at all in the joint.

Activities of Daily Living (ADL)

Besides determining the source and extent of paralysis and the limitation of joint motion, the therapist must also know how well a patient can function with whatever motion is left after a disease or injury. The therapist tests the performance of Activities of Daily Living (ADL) by observing how patients feed, bathe, and dress themselves; how they write or use a computer, handle a telephone, and maneuver a wheelchair.

EXERCISE PROGRAMS

After determining the extent of a disability, the therapist plans an exercise program to build strength and increase motion. Planning such a program to restore the patient to a productive life is the most stimulating and rewarding responsibility of a physical therapist.

Traditional Therapeutic Program

A therapeutic exercise program is much different from the calisthenics in a physical education class. Sometimes treatment begins with *passive motion,* in which the therapist moves a body part for the patient, to make the patient aware of the sensation of motion. Knowledge of the sensation is fundamental to all voluntary movement. The next step is *passive assistive motion,* in which the therapist moves the body part, with the patient helping a little. The third step is *active assistance exercise,* in which the patient moves, with the therapist offering some assistance. Next, the *patient moves without any assistance.* Last, the *patient moves against resistance* offered by a therapist or by weights attached to the arms or legs. Those who have practiced weight lifting know that muscles gain strength more quickly when they move against resistance than by moving more frequently without resistance. This pattern of exercise has been the conventional and traditional program for more than fifty years.

Advances in Recent Years

During the past sixty years, however, there have been exciting advances in therapeutic exercise. Several groups of scientists in different parts of the United States and Great Britain studied reflexes and the normal progression of motor skills in infants and young children. Through their research, physicians and physical therapists have learned that:

1. Certain sensations, such as cold, tapping, brushing, or rubbing will cause a muscle to contract when the usual progression of the conventional exercise program fails to produce motion.

2. Adults and children learn to walk more easily if they have learned to do all the things that normal infants and children do before walking. If a patient can roll over, crouch, crawl, and kneel upright, walking is less difficult.

3. Motor reflexes, certain involuntary movements over which a patient at first has no control, can be used as a foundation for teaching willed and voluntary motion.

Five systems of exercise have developed using these basic neurological and developmental principles. Each system is different from the others in its approach to the patient.

Some therapists use one system exclusively, while others take parts from all the systems to achieve results. For anyone interested in research, investigation into the vast field of motor development would be challenging to the therapist engaged in research and beneficial to all the therapists practicing in clinics.

In general hospitals, therapists frequently teach patients to walk with crutches, without placing any weight on an injured leg or by placing partial weight on a weak or painful leg. The therapist must fit the crutches to the patient, then decide which of the five crutch gaits is best for the patient. As soon as the patient can walk independently, the therapist will instruct the patient how to sit down, rise from a chair, and climb and descend stairs. Not all patients can use crutches; some never pass beyond the walker stage, while others advance quickly to a cane. Sometimes after a patient learns to walk, a therapist may teach her or him to run, skip, and perform some ballroom, folk, and modern dance movements.

Physical therapists also assist with treatment of lung diseases. British therapists have long been aware of the value of pulmonary care for patients suffering from lung congestion. In this exercise system, the patient lies in a certain position to drain the fluid from a specific lobe of the lung. While the patient is tilted, the therapist claps and vibrates (two massage techniques) over the lobe being drained. The patients also learn breathing exercises that emphasize breathing out and coughing.

Many obstetrical patients learn groups of abdominal exercises before and after the delivery of a baby. Sometimes the therapist teaches these in classes, but more frequently he or she instructs each patient independently.

In every general hospital department, therapists teach posture correction exercises to patients who have pain resulting from poor body mechanics and to youngsters who are developing bad postural habits that might produce serious deformities.

Orthopedic physical therapy is a rapidly expanding specialty. Therapists who use this treatment must learn the techniques of mobilization and manipulation used in osteopathy. The therapists who use mobilization and manipulation of joints to increase the range of motion must take many advanced courses, and they must continue to study independently and to practice constantly. This therapy requires specialized technique and knowledge, and special skill in working with the patients to create an atmosphere conducive to their complete cooperation and relaxation during the procedures. *Manual therapy,* as it is called in physical therapy, can increase range and relieve pain dramatically and rapidly, in the situations where it is indicated. Although many therapists have learned to mobilize, some have had difficulty in timing the manipulation thrust. Another technique in the same category is a form of osteopathy called "Strain and Counter Strain," which combines pressure with position to relieve pain.

Cranio-sacral therapy is another osteopathic technique to relieve pain. It, too, requires intensive postgraduate studies.

Although most of a therapist's time is spent in teaching patients to move, sometimes a therapist must teach a patient who is very tense and nervous how to relax.

Every physical therapy department has exercise equipment that a patient may use independently before or after a session with the therapist. The weights, wands, stall bars, wrist rolls, shoulder wheels, pulleys, and bicycles all emphasize the need for the patient to assume the responsibility for her or his own exercise program. The patient must not depend totally upon the therapist for improvement. Sometimes yoga positions and dance patterns are included in the exercise program.

A physical therapist uses different exercises for different disabilities, but exercises are beneficial for many conditions, including polio, cerebral palsy, hemiplegia, spinal cord injury, multiple sclerosis, muscular dystrophy, Parkinson's disease, emphysema, bronchiechtasis, cystic fibrosis, arthritis, burns, nerve and muscle lacerations, poor posture, mental illness, and the postoperative care of amputees. These exercises are also used by patients who have had corrective bone, joint, and muscle surgery.

Often, the exercise program begins in a pool or in a large tank of water. The buoyancy of the water makes movement easier, and a weak muscle can develop strength and coordination more rapidly. Sometimes patients begin walking in pools or in specially designed tanks.

THE "MODALITIES"

A word used frequently in physical therapy jargon is "modalities." Physical therapists use this word to refer to many treatments requiring large pieces of electrical equipment. The term is frowned upon by many school faculty members and many of the profession's leaders, but the clinicians working in the field continue to use it. Usually, the assistant's activities and responsibilities include these treatment procedures. If a department has no assistants, the physical therapist will administer the treatments.

Hydrotherapy

Hydrotherapy is the use of water in treatment. The water is warm, usually slightly above body temperature. The water is caused to whirl by a jet of air forced from a turbine that looks like an outboard motor but that, of course, has no rotor blades. Immediately following severe trauma (accident), however, patients, including athletes involved in sports-related injuries, are treated in very cold water.

The combination of heat and the water massage helps to relieve pain and to increase circulation. It is also beneficial in cleansing an arm or leg after a cast, splint, or dressing has been removed or when a large area of tissue has been severely burned, frostbitten, or ulcerated.

A popular and easy form of home treatment that therapists often teach patients suffering from arthritis of the hands and feet is the contrast bath, the alternating use of hot and cold water in a specific time sequence.

Paraffin Baths

Paraffin baths—the use of paraffin and mineral oil mixed together and heated to temperatures between 123 and 132 degrees Fahrenheit—provide an effective relief from the pain of arthritis and inflammation of the tendons of the hands and feet. They are also one of the mainstays of physical therapy treatment for patients with leprosy. The patient dips her or his hands into the wax about seven times, then continues to soak the hands in the wax or wraps the paraffin-coated hands in a towel for twenty to thirty minutes.

Hot Packs

Hot packs—pads containing a mixture of silicon, gelatin, and chemicals—retain heat for relatively long periods and effectively reduce pain. A thermostatically controlled cabinet keeps the packs hot until the therapist wraps them in towels and applies them to a patient.

Elastogel Packs can be heated in an oven or microwave, or frozen in a freezer, as a convenient method of conductive heat or cold.

There is some controversy regarding the relative efficacy of dry and moist heat.

Radiant Heat

Heat from an infrared lamp often precedes other procedures such as massage or exercise. Both infrared and ultraviolet rays are forms of radiant heat, but they are at opposite ends of the color spectrum, so the effects are totally different. Ultraviolet produces no heat but has instead a chemical effect upon the skin. The patient notices a mild sunburn several hours after the exposure, just as you notice a sunburn after you return from the beach. Ultraviolet is successful in the treatment of skin diseases and is especially beneficial in promoting the healing of pressure sores.

Diathermy

Diathermy is a form of heat produced by the resistance of the tissues to the short waves of an electrical current. Because the heat is a milder dosage of the same inductotherm used to melt metal in the steel mills, the diathermy cannot be used on patients who have metal implanted in their bones. Diathermy that penetrates from one-and-a-half to two inches brings great comfort to patients with aches and pains in muscles and joints.

Ultrasound

Ultrasound has proven to be an extremely effective measure in reducing pain, especially after sudden injuries such as sprains and strains. There are many other conditions that respond to sound, such as arthritis, bursitis, tendinitis, and muscular pains. More recently, sound has been successful in the treatment of warts on the sole of the foot and around nail beds of the fingers and toes.

Ultrasound waves are faster than waves in the range of human hearing, but not faster than sound; that is why they are called "ultrasound waves." Ultrasound is produced by a current of electricity passing through a transducer, or sound head, that looks something like an old pistol. Inside the transducer the current passes through a quartz crystal that changes the current into ultrasound. The physical therapist applies ultrasound by moving the transducer over the painful area. Hands and feet, which have irregular contours, may be treated underwater.

Electrical Current

You read earlier of the use of electrical current in testing muscles and nerves. These currents are also used in treatment. In one type of treatment, called *iontophoresis* or ion transfer, the current deposits chemicals or medicines on wounds or ulcers to hasten healing. The electrical current used to stimulate muscle contractions teaches the muscle to move again when it has forgotten how or when it is too weak to move voluntarily.

Direct current, called *galvanic current,* has been successful in reducing pain. For many years, high voltage was in vogue, but since 1985, the application of micro-amperage currents proved to be more successful in sports medicine and other types of trauma, as well as podiatry.

Transcutaneous Electrical Nerve Stimulation

TENS, a low volt galvanic application, is a battery-operated device with electrodes placed upon the patient in the area of pain, or on the acupoints applicable to the pain. TENS units are worn by patients who suffer from constant, chronic pain. Therapists instruct the patient in the points of application and periods of time to be used, in order to obtain relief from pain. This is primarily a "home care" modality, and rarely used in a clinical setting, except for testing its efficacy and for instruction.

Ice

During World War II, when physical therapy began to gain momentum, almost every order for treatment read, "heat, massage, and exercise."

Physiologists are still uncertain about the reason why ice is an effective method of reducing pain and spasticity. Therapists have observed that ice produces gratifying results. Patients experience almost immediate relief from pain and also an increase in motion. The therapist may apply crushed ice in a plastic or rubber bag or may massage the patient with a large chunk of ice, applying it directly to the skin until the area becomes numb. Usually, the patient receives additional instruction in the use of ice at home. Patients who are spastic because they suffer from multiple sclerosis are often submerged in a tub of ice water for four minutes. The cold water relieves the spasticity for many hours.

Traction

Many patients who suffer from pain in the low back, neck, or head receive relief from traction. The traction can be steady or intermittent. The patient may be lying down or sitting up. The traction can be applied to the lower back or to the neck with a pelvic belt or a head halter. Traction will stretch the muscles and increase circulation and often results in the correction of joint dysfunction.

Vaso-Pneumatic Pumping

Some patients have a great deal of swelling in their arms and legs from a variety of causes. They are helped by means of a device called the Intermittent Pressure unit, which forces the fluid from the extremities by pressure within a sleeve or stocking. The treatments last for varying periods of time, ranging from three to twenty-four hours a day. When the edema or swelling has gone, the therapist measures the arm or leg with special tapes, at points an inch and a half apart, for custom-made, pressure-gradient supports to give the circulatory system some help.

Massage

For centuries, in all parts of the world, massage has been a method of relieving pain, inducing relaxation, and increasing circulation. In recent years, researchers debunked some of the old theories about its results, but it remains an effective method of treatment.

Physical therapists massage to increase circulation, to relieve pain, and to stretch tight muscles. In more recent years, stretching of the fascia has become an important method of relieving areas of tissue tension. This is called *Myofascial Release,* and it can be a very painful procedure, but extremely effective.

Currently, therapists use massage techniques in the treatment of specific muscular or fascial problems. It is rare for a physical therapist to administer a complete body massage for relaxation, or "just because it feels so great."

Acu-Therapy

The Chinese began developing acupuncture treatments four thousand years ago by inserting needles into various parts of the body. The Japanese used the same concept, but used pressure and called it *Shiatsu.*

Western allopathic medicine has looked askance at this therapy for many decades, but recent research is recognizing that 70 percent of the acupoints are the myoneural junctions, and that there is a relationship of the points to the body's electrophysiology, and to the release of the endorphins and enkephalins in the brain.

The philosophy is much too complicated to detail here, but in the practice of acu-therapy, physical therapists apply an electrical current or pressure, a cold laser, or a cold spray to the acupoints. In the United States, physical therapists may not insert needles, although this is permitted in other countries. In the United States, physical therapists may use acu-therapy to relieve pain only, but not to treat disease entities.

Therapists interested in this approach to treating pain must attend continuing education courses, because it is not a part of the curriculum in the academic courses.

And Many Other Duties

During a typical day, a therapist or an assistant will do many more things than those just described. You may consult with a physician to decide the best type of brace for a patient or the height of a lift on a shoe. You might teach a patient how to put on an artificial arm or leg and how to use the prosthesis effectively. You might put dressings over wounds. In some of the large hospitals, which have burn units, physical therapists debride necrotic tissue—that is, they scrub, scrape, and cut away skin so badly burned that it is dead.

The therapist may frequently saw off canes, take photographs of unusual conditions, make splints of plaster of paris or other materials, and make permanent records of deformities of hands and feet by using finger paint and felt marking pens.

Then there are the days when the therapist mops part of the floor or changes a diaper.

THE PHYSICAL THERAPIST AS AN ADMINISTRATOR

In the early years of physical therapy, the therapist, like the doctor of earlier times, had a one-on-one relationship with patients. It was the great personal contact of "laying on of hands" and the resulting gratitude from patients that brought many people into the field in its earlier days.

Today, the average physical therapist in the United States consults with many other professionals: physicians, dentists, nurses, occupational therapists, speech-language pathologists, and audiologists. The comparatively rapid shift from the therapist's responsibility for the total care of the patient to the current role of administrator and teacher has resulted from the population explosion, the increased public demands for better health care, and expanded physical therapy treatments.

In the average hospital, a patient's physical therapy treatment requires one hour; in a rehabilitation center, the average treatment is two-and-a-half hours long. No matter how intensely the physical therapist may want to cling to the role of practicing clinician, he or she must often abandon it to become an administrator and teacher.

The Department Director

Whether by choice or by chance, the director of a department is in a position that demands great professional and personal dedication. Directors are very special kinds of leaders. They have two responsibilities: one to the hospital administration and one to their own staffs. But they must be primarily concerned with the development of the staff and with the constant improvement of the department's service.

Department directors often play many roles. They are guides, planners, overseers, evaluators, interpreters, reporters, teachers, and, sometimes, counselors, confessors, and peacemakers. In each role, they are expected to excel!

The concrete and tangible responsibilities are many and varied. They may assist in designing a desirable floor plan for a new department or decide on the new equipment that the hospital or center requires to meet the needs of the community.

Department directors cooperate with the administration, the controller, and the accounting departments in establishing a budget and working within that budget. They assist in establishing an equitable fee scale based on actual cost. They assist in preparing forms for referrals, records, billing, and inventory. They also prepare statistics and periodic reports of department activity.

They work closely with the personnel department to prepare job descriptions, personnel policies, and a just salary scale. They help to recruit and select the staff. The search for a professional physical therapy staff is relentless, because the current competition for new graduates is high. The pressure of offering continuing education opportunities and maintaining morale is constant because the turnover is steady no matter how ideal the working conditions may be.

Department directors represent the hospital administration to the physical therapy department staff and the staff to the administration. Directors attend department head meetings and relay the important information learned there. They must always insist that their staff comply with all the hospital or institution rules. On the other hand, they have an obligation to their employees to communicate unusual problems to the administration and to back just demands. This sounds as though department heads are walking a tightrope—and it often seems that way!

The director or chief therapist will attend medical staff meetings where physical therapy patients are studied and will review patients' progress for the doctors. In some hospitals, the director accompanies the doctors on ward rounds.

Teaching and Student Supervision

If a hospital has a school of nursing, the director of physical therapy may teach as a guest lecturer in such areas as body mechanics, transfer techniques, massage, crutch walking, orthopedics, and the care of the patient who has had a stroke.

In a hospital or rehabilitation center serving as an affiliating center for physical therapy students in the final phase of their professional education preparation, the department director, assistant director, or clinical supervisor supervises the students' clinical experience, criticizes, counsels, and consoles them—and prepares extensive reports on their performances. As a member of the clinical faculty of a physical therapy school, the director or a delegate will attend many of the regular faculty meetings.

In large departments, where the staff may include as many as twenty-five professional physical therapists and a greater number of subprofessional and nonprofessional workers, the director will serve only as an administrator and coordinator. The director will give no individual patient treatment and will probably designate a qualified staff member to be responsible for teaching programs. In medium-sized departments, the director may or may not give treatment; may perform only tests and certain evaluative procedures, or treat very difficult patients.

In a private practice, or in a small department, the director may be the one-person show, administering all treatments.

CHAPTER 4

PHYSICAL THERAPY WORK SETTINGS

A VARIETY OF NEEDS AND SETTINGS

When you begin the professional practice of physical therapy, your responsibility will be to the total patient, not just to a back, a knee, or a hand. You must treat the entire person—the mind and social behavior as well as the body.

All physical therapists use physical agents in the treatments they give, but there are many specialties within physical therapy because there are many different kinds of patients. There are also many different kinds of work you might do.

It would be impossible to tell you about every type of hospital, institution, agency, and specialty where physical therapists work. In this chapter, the larger categories of employment opportunities will be described. Two-thirds of physical therapists work in hospitals or physical therapy offices.

In general hospitals the care is centered around patients with acute diseases and disabilities. Some of these are admitted primarily for physical therapy and rehabilitation procedures, while others are admitted for medical or surgical care but receive physical therapy as an additional aid to recovery.

Many patients are outpatients in hospital departments or private practice offices. Nursing homes and rehabilitation centers employ physical therapists. Patients who live at home, but who are too infirm to be transported, are treated in their homes. Schools must also employ physical therapists. Sports medicine and industrial clinics are gaining in importance.

The Hospital Setting

Hospitals in big cities usually have large, well-equipped departments. The medical director might be a physiatrist (a doctor specializing in physical medicine and rehabilitation) who is on duty in the department full-time to examine all new patients, to prescribe and observe treatment and the patient's reaction to it, to change orders of other physicians, and to recommend specific types of braces and artificial limbs. There are relatively few physiatrists in our country, however. In most hospitals, an orthopedist (a bone and joint specialist) or an internist (a physician specializing in internal diseases) will serve a specific number of hours each month to review referrals, assist in the solution of difficult problems, and serve as a liaison with the medical staff. In some larger, more progressive hospitals, there has been a trend toward the establishment of a committee or board to serve as the medical consultant team. This board is usually composed of an orthopedist, a neurologist, an internist, a rheumatologist, a psychiatrist, and, if possible, a specialist in respiratory disease. The committee meets regularly with the physical therapy director to review administrative, medical, and legal problems.

Except for a very few hospitals where a physiatrist is on duty all day, the working director is the physical therapist in charge of the department. This therapist might be called "director" or "supervisor" or "chief" depending on the hospital, but whatever the title, her or his responsibilities are the same—operating an efficient department that gives every patient the best possible care.

Very large departments may have as many as thirty or thirty-five physical therapists and physical therapist assistants, while a small department may have only the chief physical therapist and one assistant. There will also be nonprofessional aides and orderlies who transport patients, make beds, sort linen, clean equipment, and fill hydrotherapy tanks. All large departments have clerk-receptionists who receive patients and direct them to the proper areas, make out bills, answer the phone, deliver messages, type routine letters and reports, and file.

In small hospitals the medical director may be an orthopedist, internist, or general practitioner serving without salary on an on-call basis. He or she may give very little supervision to the physical therapy staff and be called only in a crisis. In such a department, the chief therapist is responsible for all direct patient care and all administrative details. The small department may or may not have subprofessional, nonprofessional, and clerical staff.

The larger physical therapy departments usually have a reception room, an office, and an electrotherapy area where patients receive treatments such as diathermy, ultrasound, infrared, ultraviolet, hot packs, ice, electrical stimulation, paraffin, traction, massage, and some of the exercise programs. In the hydrotherapy area there may be a pool or a key-shaped Hubbard tank where patients lie for underwater exercises. There are usually a number of smaller whirlpools also. The gymnasium, or exercise room, has a set of parallel bars, walkers, and crutches, canes, and practice staircases for walking training. Often there are stall bars, shoulder wheels, pulleys, wrist rolls, finger ladders, wands, weights, bicycles, floor mats, and other exercise equipment, such as the Cybex unit, Orthotron, and NK table.

Many small departments consist of only one room, with one machine of each type in it, as well as the gait-training equipment and office furniture. In such a small department, every inch of space must be used to maximum efficiency.

Although the patients in general hospitals suffer from a variety of difficulties, those receiving physical therapy usually suffer from the same problems of arthritis, strokes, fractures, lacerations, ruptured discs, and other back and posture-related difficulties. In some of the larger metropolitan hospitals with many specialists, the physical therapist may treat patients with the rarer neuromuscular diseases such as multiple sclerosis, muscular dystrophy, transverse myelitis, and the Guillame-Barre syndrome, Parkinson's Disease, and post-polio syndrome.

Physical therapy also is used for patients suffering from lung diseases such as asthma and its complications, pneumonia, cystic fibrosis, and many others. Physical therapists can help these patients by instructing them in pulmonary exercises and by performing postural drainage.

In centers where there is a great deal of heart surgery performed, or where there is a cardiac care unit, the physical therapist may develop an exercise program to increase strength and endurance and to increase the amount of air the patient can inhale and exhale. Following surgery, a patient is instructed in exercises to correct posture and to increase shoulder motion.

Some skin problems, such as ulcers and burns, are treated with whirlpool, iontophoresis, hyper-baric oxygen, and ultraviolet light.

Involvement of physical therapists in obstetrics and gynecology will vary with the interest of the doctors in certain types of problems, use of natural childbirth, and postdelivery rehabilitation.

In some institutions the physical therapist works with the orthodontist on problems of the temporal mandibular joint, in facial exercises, and in correcting postural problems that are now recognized to be concurrent with some dental problems.

In some hospitals, physical therapists as well as occupational therapists treat patients in psychiatric wards.

Each hospital and department has a personality of its own. In big cities, where the crime rate is high, many gunshot and stab wound patients may receive intensive physical therapy during the rehabilitation period. In large industrial communities, the number of trauma patients from job-related injuries can be high. Many of these patients have fractures from falls, brain damage from blows to the head, and severe lacerations from machinery.

Hospitals in mining communities also treat large numbers of industrial accident cases that occur in the mines. In farming communities, hand injuries result from accidents that occur while people are feeding animals or repairing farm machinery. In sheep and cattle country, sheep herders and ranchers suffer from fractures and ruptured spinal discs from falling off horses, especially before and during rodeo season. Burns are common in areas where there are foundries and steel mills. In ski resorts there are many people with fractured legs. In the retirement areas of Florida and Arizona there are many older patients with strokes and arthritis.

In large hospitals, therapists have an excellent opportunity to attend medical staff conferences, special medical seminars, and ward rounds. They may also participate in experiments and research. Usually, physical therapy students obtain their clinical experience in the larger, better equipped hospitals in more cosmopolitan centers, so the staff in these hospitals can participate in their training program.

Therapists in small departments, in small hospitals, and in small towns see fewer rare diseases, have less opportunity to share in medical education, and have fewer opportunities to teach. They may need more imagination and initiative. A therapist in a small hospital may have to convert an area never intended for physical therapy into an efficient department. He or she will function with very little medical supervision. One rewarding difference, however, is that in a small hospital, there is a much closer relationship between all personnel.

Small hospitals, especially those in rural areas, sometimes suffer from staffing shortages. In these hospitals, a heavier caseload will require a therapist to work faster and to limit conversation with the patient. If the caseload is lighter, the therapist will have time to relate more to patients, to read, and study.

Life in the general hospital is dramatic, the pace is fast, and the patient turnover is rapid. There is more rejoicing with the patients over their rapid recovery and more pathos from unexpected deaths. There is a greater variety in diagnosis and a wider choice of treatments to administer than in the smaller hospital.

PEDIATRICS

Every child is appealing and lovable, but the handicapped and helpless child needs more than the expression of love through tender words and cuddling. He or she needs the expression of love through deeds. There is nothing more gratifying to a physical therapist than the knowledge that, through his or her efforts, a handicapped child has learned to cope better with life's problems. Perhaps this is the reason why almost every physical therapy student expresses a desire to work with children for at least a short period.

Some large cities and some smaller cities with large medical school complexes have general hospitals exclusively for children. The children may be as young as newborns or as old as twelve or fourteen. They may have acute diseases or they may have chronic conditions requiring reconstructive procedures.

Only a small percentage of the children in these hospitals require physical therapy. Many of the children receiving physical therapy in the hospitals for the acutely ill suffer from cystic fibrosis (a disease that affects many parts of the body, but especially the lungs), or they receive preoperative and postoperative care when surgery to the muscles, tendons, joints, or nerves will make motion easier and more effective.

Most children's hospitals offer programs of extended convalescent care or prolonged "habilitation" programs. The children remain in these hospitals from several weeks to several years. There are usually school programs, scout troops, and other organized social activities within the hospital.

About 25 percent of all orthopedically handicapped children require a period of hospitalization, and one-third of these live in rural areas where there are no facilities for medical care. For this reason, rural children must remain hospitalized for longer periods than children in large cities who may report for treatment to hospitals or private offices or may receive treatment in the schools.

The furniture and treatment equipment in children's hospitals are child size. Instead of walkers, the children sometimes use weighted doll buggies. Some children develop their walking skill by using skis equipped with high poles to hold. The therapist frequently treats the children on a mat on the floor rather than on a high treatment table. There is also a great deal of pool work to encourage general and specific motions.

If you were working in a children's hospital, you would discuss your treatment objectives with the nurses in each ward, so that the treatment plan would be reinforced in play time and in school sessions. You would also work closely with the occupational and speech therapists to coordinate and intensify each treatment program. When a child was ready for discharge, you would give the parents detailed instructions in the necessary exercises that they would continue at home.

PUBLIC SCHOOLS

Some metropolitan areas have special schools with specific equipment for handicapped children, while smaller communities may have one classroom housed in a regular school building. Most programs last from kindergarten through high school.

Often children return to the general classroom if they can cope with the demands. Physical therapists sometimes visit the schools to treat these special children.

All schools are required by federal law to provide special equipment so that qualified students can be successfully mainstreamed into regular education classrooms.

The primary purpose of the school for the handicapped child is education. It is not primarily a treatment center with the school program added, as is the situation in the convalescent hospital for children. The treatment program in the school is important, but it is definitely secondary to the academic program.

The same basic principles of education that are involved in teaching academic subjects apply to the teaching of a motor activity. Motivation is basic to all treatment, and the treatment must be planned to develop the child's will to improve. The physical therapist must perform testing procedures to evaluate muscle strength and range of motion. Then he or she must develop an exercise program to develop strength, coordination, balance, and Activities of Daily Living (ADL) skills. If you worked in a school, you would also share with the doctor the responsibility of fitting and maintaining the children in braces, artificial limbs, or other special equipment.

Therapists working in children's programs must possess ingenuity and initiative as well as the knowledge of basic physical therapy principles and procedures. They must correlate the technique with the use of equipment and must often adapt the furniture such as chairs, desks, and wheelchairs to fit the needs of specific children. Mechanical aptitude is a great asset here.

Like the teachers in a school, therapists must share in other activities of the school. They attend staff meetings and conferences to interpret the capability and disability of the child in the classroom. Therapists share the philosophy of rehabilitation with the entire school faculty and assist them in the management of the child. Therapists also share in the responsibility for such nonphysical therapy duties as fire drills, bus duty, educational trips, and safety programs. Therapists usually serve on the committee to help screen children for admission to the special school and again to recommend transfer of children to regular schools.

Since the effectiveness of the program depends on parental cooperation, a great deal of this work involves parent instruction, demonstration, and conferences to interpret the child's changing needs, and the therapies used to meet them.

In the school programs, the physical therapist is employed by the board of education or the board of health, by a private agency, or by the city as a civil servant. Whatever agency pays the salary, the therapist is entitled to all the benefits and privileges that teachers enjoy—annual salary increments, sick leave, retirement benefits, and summer vacations.

In a typical school the therapist treats between 8:30 A.M. and 3:30 P.M., Monday through Friday, from September until June. During these nine months, the therapist shares with the academic faculty of the school the job of watching children grow. Like the teachers of handicapped children, the physical therapist needs a great love for children and enthusiasm and patience. Because the therapists are away from professional colleagues while working in a school environment, they must possess added self-discipline to continue their own professional education.

INDUSTRIAL CLINICS

Some large companies have small but well-equipped physical therapy departments in their dispensaries in order to return injured employees to their jobs in the best possible condition and in the shortest possible time following an injury.

Twenty-five percent of these injuries are hand injuries, but many are multiple injuries involving fractures, sprains, strains, dislocations, crush injuries, lacerations, amputations, ruptured muscles and nerves, and weakness resulting from injuries.

The turnover of patients in these industrial clinics is rapid because no chronic conditions are treated and much of the work is preventive. The caseload is heavy; the tempo of the work is fast. The therapist working in industrial clinics must enjoy working largely with men and must be diplomatic, yet able to prod the patient on to harder work. He or she must be able to organize a volume of work well.

Because there are many lawsuits filed by employees following industrial accidents, the industrial therapist must keep detailed and extensive records of progress and make frequent appearances in court.

Ergonomics is a new and rapidly expanding area in industrial medicine.

Approximately ten years ago, the Volvo automobile factory in Sweden became alarmed by the number of industrial related accidents, and began a program to prevent, rather than to treat, injuries. The program was so successful that other nations have copied it.

Therapists involved in this type of program will inspect equipment for the placement, height, comfort, and other parameters, to minimize the workers' strain. The therapist will also conduct classes on body mechanics and often conduct Back Schools, on the company premises.

Ergonomics became the most rapidly expanding specialty in physical therapy in the 1990s because it resulted in a great decrease in injuries and in cost.

GERIATRICS

Institutions for the care of the aged are growing, both in size and number. Some older patients cannot return home because of the severity of a stroke or arthritis or the aftereffects of a fracture. Others cannot return simply because there is no one at home to care for them during the convalescent period after a fracture or operation.

Many older patients receive heat, massage, exercises, walking training, and self-help activities to make them independent. The therapist may administer this treatment directly or teach other members of the hospital or nursing home staff to do this work with the patients.

The pace in a geriatrics center is slower because the patients move slower. They need more time for repetition of movement and more time to talk about their problems. In the geriatric setting, the therapist must stress the psychological aspects of care as much as the actual and physical care. He or she must emphasize the individuality of the patient and must strive constantly to reestablish the patient's self-confidence. The therapist must be on guard not to promise unrealistic goals to the weary older person.

In some of the larger institutions a staff of qualified physical therapists is on hand to treat and to supervise treatments. In many institutions, however, the physical therapist serves as a consultant.

Salaries in the geriatric field tend to be higher than those in general hospital work and in some phases of pediatrics, because this area of treatment and care has less emotional appeal than many others.

Physical therapy departments in rehabilitation centers and curative workshops are similar to those in general hospitals treating a majority of orthopedic and neurological patients. In some centers, the patients live at home and commute by private or public transportation or by agency-operated buses. In other centers, the patients are residents at the center.

The actual physical therapy stresses strengthening and stretching exercises, balance, and coordination training. In this respect, it is similar to all the other aspects of physical therapy. It differs from hospital work, however, in the amount of contact that the therapist has with the patient's family and the contact with representatives of other agencies in the field of health, education, and welfare. The therapist has less medical supervision, and, therefore, must plan more carefully for the patient's continued treatment program. He or she must also arrange for the patient's return to the doctor at the proper intervals.

Like the therapists in schools, those in rehabilitation centers must make adaptive equipment and must have teaching skill and the ability to motivate the patient to greater challenges and success. The physical therapist must assist the business office in ascertaining the cost of treatment and help the social service staff determine the patient's ability to pay for the services.

In rehabilitation centers, the team approach to treatment is more important than any independent form of treatment. All the services unite to treat the patient as a whole, to restore function, and to aid in psychological adjustment. Many of the disabled who seek treatment in rehabilitation centers have conditions beyond the help of definitive medical care. These patients need a dynamic and coordinated program to teach them to live effectively within the limits of their disability, but to the maximum of their capabilities. The rehabilitation process continues until the patient attains the greatest possible degree of independence, not only physically but also socially, mentally, economically, and vocationally.

PRIVATE PRACTICE

Ever since World War I, a few physical therapists have chosen to work in the offices of orthopedists, psychiatrists, and rheumatologists, for a specified salary and guaranteed fringe benefits. A very few others have chosen to be self-employed.

During the past two decades, there has been an increasing trend toward physical therapists developing private practices. In some states there had been a movement to force all therapists to be independent and to work in private practice, or in contractual agreements with large institutions and nursing homes, rather than as employees. The reason for this was an attempt to enhance the image of physical therapists as professionals.

Currently two-thirds of physical therapists work in hospitals or office settings. One-third work in home health, outpatient rehabilitation centers, nursing homes, clinics, or are self-employed. Some are part of a consulting group. Most physical therapists in private practice treat patients in a private office. These therapists must pay all their own expenses: rent, electricity, gas, telephone, and so on. They must buy all their own equipment, and they must pay their employees. They must also make arrangements for vacation and sick-leave replacements.

The treatments they give are most frequently whirlpool, hot packs, ultrasound, diathermy, traction, massage, and therapeutic exercise. Most treatments average between thirty and forty-five minutes per patient, and most patients receive three treatments a week. The average private patient receives a total of eleven treatments, but 25 percent require more than fifteen treatments. The physical therapist in private practice works between eight and thirteen hours each day, but ten hours a day is the average. Therapists in private practice treat an average of twenty patients per day. Although the physical therapist in private practice works longer hours, her or his income can be much higher than that of therapists working in hospitals or for agencies and institutions.

A major reason for developing a private practice is the potentially higher income than is possible when working for a hospital, institution, or agency. Private practice also provides for greater freedom in structuring time. Obviously, the financial risk is greater, but so are the rewards of success.

Although this type of physical therapy career is more financially rewarding, it lacks much of the excitement and personal and social contact of a hospital. It lacks the opportunity for participation in medical staff meetings and for the training of students.

A physical therapist needs at least three years' and preferably five years' experience before beginning a private practice. Therapists who leave facilities after a successful experience there and establish a practice in the same area have an easier time than those who organize a practice where they are unknown.

The success of a therapist in private practice depends on many things—the size of the community, the number of doctors, the industrial enterprises, and the number of competing departments in the area. It depends upon the attitude and the interest of local doctors in physical therapy. The ultimate success of a therapist depends, however, on the quality and quantity of his or her work, and on initiative, personality, and sales ability.

Some therapists who are self-employed in private practice have contractual arrangements with small hospitals and nursing homes. These small institutions, with between forty-five and two-hundred beds, cannot afford the expense of a physical therapy department. They therefore arrange for a private therapist to spend a certain number of hours or days each week in evaluating, testing, and developing treatment programs for the patient. The therapist must also teach the nurses, nursing assistants, aides, and orderlies how to perform certain follow-up care.

THE CONSULTANT

Since the Social Security Act of 1965 authorized Medicare, the demand for physical therapists in nursing homes and extended care facilities has far exceeded the supply. To meet the need, physical therapists formed a new group within their field called *consultants*. Consultants must have a minimum of two years of clinical practice, but most have had longer work experience in a variety of situations, including teaching and supervising.

The consultant must organize the physical therapy department, order equipment, arrange for clinical evaluations, develop treatment programs, outline them in writing, and teach the permanent staff. They make frequent reports to the referring doctors and to the administration about the department's growth and finances.

In some areas, consultants work out of a central hospital, visiting the surrounding satellite hospitals. Other areas where consultants work today are public health departments, visiting nurse associations, regional health programs, heart programs, and many other agencies.

Some consultants are self-employed and work under contract, but others are on salary. The fee arrangement will vary, depending on the locality and working hours.

HOME HEALTH CARE

A patient who is chronically ill or permanently handicapped sometimes can leave a general hospital earlier and return home if he or she has follow-up physical therapy care at home. Other patients may be able to stay out of hospitals if they can receive physical therapy in their homes. For some patients who cannot walk or who have other physical or emotional handicaps that make treatment in an ordinary department difficult or impossible, treatment in the home is necessary. A few patients lack transportation, and others must travel so far that the value of the treatment is counteracted by the difficult journey. A partial solution for these patients is treatment in the home.

The physical therapist has an obligation to serve as many people as possible, and one cannot ignore the many for the few. A home-care program is costly in time and productivity by comparison to treatment in a center. For this reason, a home-care program must be a teaching program, limited in time. It continues only long enough for the patient to adapt to the disability and for the family to learn their role in positioning and exercising the patient and adapting the furniture and the house to the patient's needs.

The therapist must decide at the outset upon the best type of treatment for the patient. Does the patient require a dynamic rehabilitation program to improve his or her condition? Is the patient a candidate for maintenance or supportive care—an exercise program that will keep the patient in the same place because the condition won't improve but should not become worse? Does the patient need only custodial care to prevent muscles and joints from getting stiff and the skin from breaking down into pressure sores?

After the therapist has decided what type of care the patient needs, it is necessary to instruct the family in the exercise program. If the patient needs a dynamic program, the therapist may bring along portable equipment, such as heat lamps, diathermy machines, ultrasound units, or weights to hasten the recovery period.

In a home-bound program, the physical therapist helps the patient to adapt to her or his disability and live with it. Therapists do more than merely give treatments, because they must help the patient and family solve the problems of the patient. They must establish a rapport with the family, and they are frequently the family's only continuing contact with the doctor.

Changes in Medicare and Private Insurance

The *home health care,* or *domiciliary service,* as it is called in the United Kingdom, has changed radically in recent years. Several decades ago when the physical therapist shortage was acute, most physical therapists employed in hospitals moonlighted evenings and weekends, to treat patients requiring ongoing care. When the private practices developed, the self-employed physical therapists included home visits with their services, because the few agencies providing home treatment, such as the Visiting Nurse Association and the Arthritis and Rheumatism Foundation, could not meet the demand.

With the recent revisions in Medicare and the rules now dictated by third-party and private insurance companies, patients are being discharged from hospitals earlier than ever before. As a result, the number of agencies sponsoring home health care programs has multiplied at a very rapid rate.

Some of these agencies are sponsored by large drug manufacturers; others are owned by other private interests. Many large metropolitan hospitals that vowed they would never become involved in home health care are developing programs to provide treatment and to prevent further loss of income. The competition for this patient population is becoming intense. The employment possibilities for this type of treatment are expanding constantly.

A therapist must have an automobile to treat home-bound patients. Although it is possible to use public transportation, it is very impractical. The number of patients a therapist treats will vary with the distance, driving time, and severity of the patients' problems. In 1996, the average salary for a physical therapist in home health was $60,000. A few commercial hospitalization policies provide coverage for home health care, but the majority do not.

INSTITUTIONS FOR THE MENTALLY ILL AND MENTALLY RETARDED

The goal of physical therapy in a hospital for the mentally ill is to keep the patient in continued contact with reality. The therapist provides patients with activities that may help them return to society as soon as possible in the best possible condition.

Some patients with schizophrenia suffer from catatonia, a condition of marked muscular rigidity resulting in contractures at the joints. Usually the patients with catatonia assume rigid, unchanging positions for extended periods of time. Physical therapists attempt to keep the joints free and the muscles limber. Many of these patients also develop pressure sores from lack of movement. The therapist attempts to stimulate the patient into changing positions and frequently must treat these pressure areas with various modalities. Other patients develop swollen legs, and the therapist encourages these patients to move and to elevate their legs. In all of these conditions, the therapist treats the patient just as any other patient who did not have mental illness.

Specific treatments help patients overcome the problems that are confining them. Sometimes the patient lies in a sedative tub to relax. Other patients may be encouraged to play water polo to relieve their aggression or their abundance of energy. Another form of physical therapy treatment for the mentally ill patient is the salt glow, a vigorous massage in which salt is used instead of a lubricant to stimulate circulation.

The therapist working in a mental hospital must be gentle, kind, and able to understand the patient. He or she must be able to handle the patients in a firm but just manner. A therapist working in this setting must be sincere because these patients can sense very quickly when a person is indifferent or insincere. Tact, diplomacy, and an understanding of the fears of these patients are prime requisites for this job.

TREATING THE BLIND

Physical therapists play a primary role in the rehabilitation of the blind. Physical therapists do not function alone in this important work, but join with representatives from several other professional groups who work together to increase the independence of the sightless.

The physical therapist is chiefly concerned with teaching the patient an awareness of body image so that the sightless person can identify position in space, can maintain good balance, and can acquire sufficient coordination to cope with sudden changes in position while moving in a dark world.

Many sightless people have poor posture, which can result in discomfort or pain because of poor body alignment. The therapist emphasizes the importance of good posture through corrective exercises.

It is only when the blind person has developed spatial perception, good coordination, and balance that he or she can learn to move about and travel independently.

SPORTS MEDICINE

Team sports have become big business. Whether a professional team plays to earn money for the owners or a varsity team plays to enhance their school's image, all individuals on the team have a serious obligation to fulfill their assignments.

The player must be in the best possible condition before the game. If injured during the game, he or she must receive the best treatment possible as quickly as possible to return to active competition.

Injuries are more common among high school and college athletes than among the professionals. The amateur, who is primarily a student, does not have adequate time to devote to the necessary conditioning before competition and consequently is much more prone to injuries.

Although most accidents occur in football, soccer, and hockey—the more aggressive sports—injuries do occur in baseball and basketball.

Both amateur and professional teams have trainers who assist in the conditioning program but are more concerned with the care of the player following injury. In the past, trainers were former athletes who had acquired a smattering of knowledge about the treatment of trauma and orthopedic injuries.

Today, this trainer is being replaced by a qualified physical therapist who has a good foundation in anatomy and kinesiology and, therefore, is better prepared to supervise the exercise program. More importantly, the physical therapist has more knowledge about treatment techniques following fractures, lacerations, sprains, strains, dislocations, and torn cartilages in the knees than has the retired athlete.

The physical therapist treats the injured player after referral by the team physician or another specialist, just as in a hospital, rehabilitation center, or in a private office.

The pace of life and work is fast. The job is an exciting one because the physical therapist travels with the team to all their engagements. The patients are young, strong, and healthy, so the outlook of the therapist is constantly optimistic. Besides being exciting and fun, the salaries in this specialty are relatively high.

Dance has grown in popularity in recent years, and today people of all ages are studying ballet and modern dance. Dancers can suffer from injuries just as serious as players in competitive sports. In ballet, the dancer assumes positions that stretch muscles and joints far beyond normal limits. Injuries to the feet, ankles, and knees are common. Some of the large dance companies have orthopedists and physical therapists on their staffs to treat the injuries of the ballet dancers.

Modern dance puts less strain on the feet and legs, but the leaps and falls can be hazardous.

A new subcategory of sports medicine or sports therapy is music therapy. Many musicians suffer from sprains and strains in the upper extremities because of the intensive use of the arms while playing instruments. For the lovers of music, this would be a rewarding experience.

Opportunities in sports medicine are exploding. Many physical therapists hold concurrent certificates as athletic trainers, and this enhances the job potential for them. Remember, too, that the Olympic teams also employ physical therapists.

FOREIGN ASSIGNMENTS

If you are blessed or cursed with an incurable wanderlust—become a physical therapist! In every nation of the world there are opportunities to live and work as a physical therapist within the culture of the country and to learn its language, religion, philosophy, and social customs while you work at your job.

If you want work experience in a certain nation, it is possible to obtain reciprocity (permission to work) if the other nation is a member of the World Confederation for Physical Therapy and if the government of that nation permits foreigners to hold salaried positions.

In Europe, where the ratio of physical therapists to the population is much greater than it is in the United States, the salaries of physical therapists are lower. It is also well to remember that the cost of living in most of the European nations is just as high or higher than the cost of living in America.

The greatest need for physical therapists is in Africa, Asia, and South America. Therapists who work on any of these three continents find problems similar to those found at home and others that are very different. Language differences present the greatest problem. In Hindu and Muslim areas, male therapists may not treat female patients, and in some Muslim areas, even foreign women may not examine or treat a Muslim woman's legs. In all of the emerging nations, there is a great deal of leprosy, tuberculosis, polio, meningitis, and other diseases (which were rampant in the United States at the turn of the century). There is relatively little work done in cerebral palsy, in geriatrics, or in the treatment of chronic problems.

Foreign assignments are exciting, but they were not created for the opportunist who merely wants to use a work assignment abroad as a springboard to a free world tour. People who request help need the guidance of therapists who are dedicated to physical therapy, their patients, and their employers. The therapists who are chosen must be mature enough and unselfish enough to work long hours, side by side with the nationals, in the heat or the cold, teaching and helping them in a true spirit of humility and good fellowship. American therapists serving abroad should attempt to live as much as possible as the people in the area live and not demand special or unusually luxurious accommodations at the expense of their hosts.

No matter where you go or under whose auspices you work, you will need a passport, visas, and an international health certificate, and it is good to have an international driver's license. You will need to be immunized against typhoid, typhus, tetanus, cholera, malaria, polio, and any other disease afflicting the nation where you will live.

Before you leave the United States, you should take time to study the history, geography, religion, social customs, and, if possible, the language of the nation where you will work.

Living conditions vary. Some organizations will provide you with luxurious accommodations, quite palatial by comparison to the community. Others offer little more than hovels. You may have servants, but you may prefer to care for your own needs.

Most people who have worked in a foreign assignment have at one time, at least, gnashed their teeth in frustration over their inability to effect more rapid change. No matter who sponsored you, you are an unofficial diplomat of the United States. You must therefore hide your irritation and remember that the reason you are there is to help relieve suffering and promote good health, regardless of national or cultural differences.

In January 1956, the World Health Organization awarded official status to the World Confederation for Physical Therapy. This placed on the World Confederation the responsibility of giving WHO technical assistance through consultation and service by providing personnel and demonstrating programs in rehabilitation. WHO also requires that the World Confederation give continuing assistance to these programs after they are started. Therapists selected for the projects are chosen from all member nations on a percentage basis.

The International Red Cross has sent physical therapists into several areas, but perhaps one of the most exciting assignments in their history was that of sending European, Australian, and American therapists to Morocco in 1960, when thousands of people became paralyzed after consuming contaminated cooking oil. The therapists screened the patients, tested them, and taught Moroccan assistants how to exercise them.

TEACHING

There have been many changes in physical therapy education during the past thirty years. The earlier schools were attached to hospitals, and the instructors were usually part of the hospital physical therapy staff who taught techniques after the doctors laid the foundation in anatomy, physiology, and medical lectures.

The university program today has brought a sharp differentiation between the role of the teacher in the academic institution and the role of the practicing clinician. In the physical therapy schools today, all faculty members must have a master's degree, and a doctorate is necessary for school directors.

The emphasis today is on the *why* of physical therapy, rather than on the *how* of four or five decades ago. The teachers planning the curricula must provide each student with opportunities to obtain a broad knowledge of anatomy, physiology, pathology, kinesiology, neurology, orthopedics, and medical principles, as well as proficiency in physical therapy techniques.

The university faculty of today accept as a part of its responsibility research in the field. Teachers must be constantly concerned with changes in the profession and must anticipate the needs of the future and adjust the curriculum to meet the demands.

There are two types of faculty members. One is the academic, full-time faculty member who teaches classroom subjects and is paid a salary by the university according to his or her position.

The other type of faculty member is called "clinical faculty member." These physical therapists work with students in the practical application of their knowledge. At various periods during the academic course and at the completion of it, the academic faculty arranges for the students to spend time in approved clinical settings, where well-qualified physical therapists observe, teach, and critique the students. Clinical faculty members rarely receive compensation other than the privilege of taking one free course each semester.

Opportunities in physical therapy education are exciting; the responsibilities, however, can be burdensome, but the educational process is fascinating. To be a part of this process can be stimulating and challenging, and observing its result can hold many rewards.

RESEARCH AND WRITING

The rate of growth in any profession depends upon the amount of information that research contributes to the profession. Physical therapy began as a service to patients, not as a body of knowledge. Research came later and grew up on the fringe of the practice of physical therapy.

Today, both in the academic halls and in busy clinics, therapists consider the how, the where, the why, and the when of the treatments that they have given for so many years. This systematic investigation of physical therapy is long overdue. Physical therapists must clarify what needs to be known and thus better prepare students for more extensive research in both science and in practice.

The physical therapist in research must cooperate with all the members of the rehabilitation team, but therapists must no longer rely upon other related bodies of learning to supply their knowledge. Specific research problems of physical therapy as distinct from other areas such as nursing, psychology, and orthopedics, are now receiving professional, focused, research attention. Those who wish to learn how to research must enroll in proper courses in the large universities and join forces with the established investigators so they may learn and employ the necessary skills.

Writing the results of research is important because it informs others of the results. Physical therapists must reevaluate old material in the light of new knowledge and experience, read widely, and study the current literature carefully. They must report even minor tips in the practice of physical therapy that might help their fellow workers. They should report illustrative cases.

In short, in both research and writing, a physical therapist must give old ideas a new examination, and work steadily toward the growth of the body of physical therapy research literature needed today.

CHAPTER 5

GETTING STARTED

Most physical therapy schools suggest that new graduates accept positions in large teaching hospitals in metropolitan areas. This is not mandatory, of course, but a position offering a variety of experiences will help you decide in which area of physical therapy you want to specialize.

If you decide to join the armed forces or the U.S. Public Health Service, you will apply directly to these and accept the post they assign you. If you decide upon a position in civilian life, however, you must make several choices before beginning to look for a job.

You must decide which is more important to you—a job in a particular hospital or living in a certain locality. Must you live in Boston, New York, or San Francisco? Do you want to make your home in a ski center in Colorado or a sailing area such as New England? Do you yearn for the perpetual summer of Arizona and Florida?

After you decide, you will begin looking for the job just right for you. Many new graduates accept positions in hospitals where they received a part of their clinical experience. These institutions are teaching hospitals and offer the new graduate excellent learning opportunities. The department director and the clinical faculty know the students and can

observe which students are best fitted for the job requirements. Clinical students know which hospital has the type of
cases that interest them most and the department structure
that will help them perfect their knowledge. Students who
wish jobs in such a hospital usually apply for their positions
during their periods of clinical experience. They may be
invited to join the staff of the clinical facility during their
affiliation or very shortly after they leave it.

Some institutions delegate either a physical therapist or a
personnel officer to interview students on college campuses.
Students who are fortunate enough to attend the annual physical therapy conference in the summer may request interviews
during the week of the convention. All physical therapy
schools have lists of positions available. These are compiled
from letters sent to them by hospitals and institutions who
need therapists. The national office of the American Physical
Therapy Association supplies lists of employment opportunities to its members.

The American Physical Therapy Association also main-
tains a placement service at a local level. The national organization is divided into chapters, usually by states. Large or
heavily populated states are further divided into districts.
Each state has a placement committee with a chairperson. If
the state chapter is divided into districts, each district has a
placement committee and chairperson. These chairs keep
up-to-date listings of all positions available at the area. They
supply the list to any member of the American Physical
Therapy Association. This service is free to both the recruiting institution and the physical therapist.

If you have always had a great yearning to work in a certain hospital or certain town, but find no opening listed,

don't despair. Write to the hospital or to the organizations in the area. Few facilities are completely staffed, and the turnover is rapid enough in most departments that a job might very well open up for you. Remember, too, that many institutions with openings run advertisements only periodically and then wait for applicants. Some smaller hospitals who need staff just sit back and wait for a miracle—like you. They have learned that advertising isn't always effective.

JOB HUNTING

Job hunting is an adventure, and it can be fun. It shouldn't frighten you. Remember, everyone who has a job once hunted for it, even the directors of physical therapy departments.

Unless you accept a position in one of the hospitals where you received your clinical experience, you will have to begin job hunting. Start by writing to the directors of the departments where you would like to work. Submit a resume. Give several dates when you would be available for an interview. Occasionally therapists have been employed sight unseen, but this is rare. Most directors prefer to interview prospective staff members.

THE INTERVIEW

You should arrive for your interview equipped with pen, Social Security number, names and addresses of references, dates of previous employment, a copy of your resume, and perhaps a transcript of your college courses. When you complete the application form, don't hesitate to include jobs you have held that were not directly related to physical therapy. Working as a waitress, typist, or camp counselor may not make you a better therapist, but it will make you a better employee because someone else has polished your rough edges.

Interviewers are impressed by many things. If you have graduated from an approved school, you will be qualified for a job; whether you get the job depends upon you.

Manners are as important as knowledge. Don't sit down until you are invited; then sit, don't flop or sprawl. Don't answer questions in monosyllables because you are scared, but also don't chatter needlessly. Speak with good grammar, good diction, and in a well-modulated voice.

Good work experience is more important than a few dollars more a week. In discussing the job with the interviewer, you have a right to inquire about the working conditions, but stress your eagerness to find a job where you will learn to be a better therapist. Your first job is your most important one. You are inexperienced, impressionable, and vulnerable. If you are only interested in the size of the paycheck and the length of the vacation, you may find yourself in a job nobody else wanted.

At the conclusion of the interview, the human resources representative will probably tell you that you will be notified by mail, if your references have been satisfactory. If you have had ten interviews, you may well receive ten job offers. Obviously, you can only accept one. Today it is a job hunter's market in physical therapy. The demand far exceeds the supply. If you succeeded in getting into the physical therapy curriculum and staying through graduation, you will have many opportunities for positions.

CHOOSING THE RIGHT JOB

As soon as you decide which job you will accept, notify the director of the department. Then, either phone or write all the other institutions where you applied to inform them that you have accepted another position. Physical therapy directors will want you to survey all the positions that interest you, but they cannot hold a job open indefinitely.

As you graduate, you are a professional, and as a professional, you now have responsibilities to others. In a field as short-supplied as physical therapy is today, have the courtesy to notify the directors that they may take you off the list so they can resume recruiting other applicants.

It is very important that you select a job that is well suited to you. Often, the young therapist who performs poorly is unhappy because the work situation is not suited to her or his ability or personality. Some people have a flair for working with children but lack the patience to handle geriatric patients; others are just the opposite. Some can perform outstanding work in a well-staffed center where the workload is light and the therapists have unlimited time to devote to a few patients. These people in understaffed and busy clinics may be frustrated, morose, and often inefficient.

Often, the tone of the department makes the difference in the successful performance of physical therapists. Some prefer to work where there is close and direct supervision by a physician or by the director and where the rules are clearly defined and strictly enforced. Others would rather work where they have free rein to use their imaginations, to improvise, and to make decisions within the framework of the rules of the profession.

It is important for all of us to heed the advice of Polonius in *Hamlet.* Polonius tells his son Hamlet, "To thine ownself be true." This is as important in life as it is on a stage; as important today as it was in the sixteenth century. Recognize your abilities and your limitations, your likes and dislikes, and find the job that appeals to you. Don't play the martyr and work in a job just because someone is needed, knowing that you don't like working with a certain age group or a certain type of disability—or that you can't stand the boss. If you accept a job you really don't want, you will be personally unhappy, you will hate your job, you will reject your profession, and you will be a failure. If you choose a job you want, it will challenge you to make great contributions to your profession and to your community. Moreover, you will find yourself a bigger and better person because of it.

LEGAL AND PROFESSIONAL REQUIREMENTS

Educational and professional qualifications for physical therapists were established by the American Physiotherapy Association in 1920. In the 1930s, the American Registry of Physiotherapists established its standards. During the years between 1920 and 1950, most hospitals and institutions required their physical therapists to be members of either or both organizations, because this membership meant that the therapists had completed an acceptable course in physical therapy and had passed a very difficult examination to qualify for registration.

In the early 1940s unqualified, poorly trained people were beginning to call themselves physical therapists. At the same time, some states were putting therapists into categories with limited practitioners not recognized by the medical profession. One state, as the ancient Chinese did also, classified physical therapists with barbers.

LICENSURE

Some time ago, it became increasingly apparent that licensing would be necessary in order to establish standards of performance, because incompetence in this field is a threat to public safety. Following the hallowed tradition of state's rights, each state enacted its own licensing laws, complete with standards and regulations. Proof of graduation from an approved physical therapy school and the successful completion of the examination provided by the state are the usual criteria for licensure.

The American Physical Therapy Association is endeavoring to establish nationwide standards of competence for physical therapists. In 1953, this organization contracted with the Professional Examination Service of the American Public Health Association for the construction and maintenance of an examination. This test is now the qualifying examination for state licensure in almost all states.

THE APTA-PES TEST

The APTA-PES test is a well-constructed, up-to-date examination prepared by professionally active physical therapists with the guidance of professional examiners. The test contains multiple choice questions and is divided into three parts. Part I covers the basic sciences, part II covers the clinical sciences, and part III covers theory and procedures. The test is given in one day, in three periods totaling seven hours.

The test is usually given in the state capital, but other areas may be designated. A therapist who has taken the test may choose to have the results listed in the Interstate Reporting Service and kept on permanent file, to be sent to any state upon request. You may wish to be licensed only in the state where you are tested; or you may ask for reciprocity for one specific state.

State licensing fees are variable. In some they are nominal, but in others the cost is relatively expensive because of legal fees involving state licensure and amendments.

The American Registry of Physical Therapists was disbanded in 1970. For approximately forty years it had functioned as an examining board to qualify physical therapists and, during that time, members encountered no problems in seeking employment in many different states. When state licensure became mandatory, the ARPT no longer fulfilled its purpose and was abolished. The American Congress of Physical Medicine, which had supervised the ARPT during its existence, continued to publish a monthly journal called *The Archives of Physical Medicine.*

It is a requirement for therapists to be licensed in the fifty states. It is important for every therapist to belong to professional organizations and to participate wholeheartedly in their activities. Being a professional person means many things. It means dedication to the profession by investing money in dues to assume your share of the operating expenses and an investment of your time to promote the objectives of your organization. It is unfair to expect other therapists to work and pay while you ride along on their coattails to benefit from their efforts.

MALPRACTICE INSURANCE

Most hospitals pay the cost of malpractice insurance for physical therapists in their inclusive insurance policies. Physical therapists in private practice and in some agencies must purchase their own insurance protection. The rates vary with the type of work that a therapist engages in. This is a problem that you need not consider until you are actually employed. Malpractice suits against physical therapists are increasing, just as are those against physicians; the possibility of a lawsuit must be on the mind of the therapist constantly.

ADVANCEMENT

A new graduate usually takes a position as a staff therapist in a large hospital in an urban community. After a year or two you have proven your worth and may be promoted to a position of senior therapist, where you will assume a greater share of professional and supervisory responsibilities. If you remain in that position, you may eventually receive an appointment as assistant chief, chief, or director. Most young therapists, however, prefer to look for a different position after a year or two. This is often the position of assistant in a small department. After another year or two of experience, the therapist seeks a position as the only therapist in a very small department or as a chief in a small department. With this added experience, the position of director of a large department is within reach. A therapist who wants to establish a private practice should have varied experience in several departments before beginning to work with little or no professional supervision. Although it is not a requirement, it is wise for new graduates to work for at least a year in a large general hospital. The specialties teach a great deal, but all this knowledge is founded on general experience.

Today, an ambitious, eager, and dedicated therapist, even though comparatively young and inexperienced, may rise very quickly to a position of responsibility and prestige. The old Welsh proverb says, "The cream always rises to the top." The exceptionally well-qualified person will be singled out for promotions, for better positions, and for offices in professional organizations. The indifferent, lackadaisical, or negative personality will remain in a rut, plodding through life with neither challenge nor reward.

Of course, not everyone wants to be a chief in a large department. Many therapists want only to devote themselves to the service of humanity or to do research in one of the specialties. This need is great, and the service they give is important. Remember, even in physical therapy we need more braves than chiefs, so never look down on therapists who are not department directors.

PROFESSIONAL ORGANIZATIONS

The American Physical Therapy Association is a national association of physical therapists formed in 1921 to standardize the developing education and service of physical therapists. This organization continues to define the function of physical therapists and to promote standards of service by developing educational requirements. In addition, it aids in planning the development of new facilities and the organization, administration, and curricula of new physical therapy schools. The American Physical Therapy Association also promotes legislation for the membership and health and welfare programs. It promotes and protects the economic and general welfare of its members, and it represents those members as the spokesperson with allied professional and governmental groups.

The APTA is divided into chapters, usually comprised of states. Each chapter has a president and an executive board of the officers. Some large states have more than one chapter, while other large states prefer to divide into districts. Districts, like chapters, have officers, committees, and committee chairs. The smaller chapters and districts hold monthly meetings, which usually combine a business meeting with an educational program. Most chapters and districts sponsor evening and weekend workshops at cost for the members. Each year the chapters hold a two- to three-day conference combining business sessions, lectures, and recreational programs.

The APTA publishes a monthly journal, *The Physical Therapy Journal.* It contains articles written by members, scientists, and physicians. The APTA also publishes the *Progress Report* and the *PT Bulletin.*

PERSONAL QUALIFICATIONS

Everyone in a profession is eager to advance as rapidly as possible. Promotions and advancement bring salary increases, prestige, and greater opportunity; "Nothing succeeds like success."

Success in physical therapy depends a great deal on how well suited you are to the field. Although there is no "typical" physical therapy personality type, personal qualifications make the difference between an outstanding therapist and an ordinary one, even though the two might have had identical educational training.

Dr. James Conant said, "Ideals, like stars, can never be reached, but we use them to chart our course." Several authors have written about the necessary qualities of a physical therapist, and Katherine Worthingham *et al.*, in an article entitled "The Selection and Education of the Physical Therapy Student," give us excellent suggestions for the qualifications for a physical therapist.

> Every physical therapist must have the ability to become
> a good teacher who can help the patient help himself. The

physical therapist must be capable of communicating with the patient and his family and must be able to draw information from the patient, to hear what he has to say, and to listen to the patient with silent understanding.

Good physical therapists take responsibility for helping to build their profession as well as their own personal future. They will not submit to routine or uninspired performance of duties, but will participate in research activities, as well as assuming responsibility for their share of the rehabilitation work.

Physical therapists must like people regardless of size, weight, color, creed, income level, or disposition. They must have friendly, kind, and patient personalities. They must be sympathetic, but not possess maudlin sympathy that destroys the working relationship. They must be dignified but not stuffy. They must have the emotional stability to be professional persons who perform their obligations during working hours without letting their personal lives interfere with their work. By the same token, they must not become so involved with their patients that they carry their patients' problems into their own personal lives. Their personalities must be both mature and flexible, so that they can vary the programs they administer; they must not let themselves become automatons.

Good working habits are especially important in careers that require both a knowledge of scientific subjects and the ability to deal effectively with people. Physical therapists must be industrious, conscientious, neat, clean, punctual, attentive to details, and able to concentrate completely on their work. They must be able to organize a schedule because most departments carry heavy workloads. It is important that they keep accurate records and be meticulously honest with themselves and others.

Physical therapists must possess leadership to influence those who look to them for guidance and support. They must also feel pride in accomplishment. To perform at the highest levels, they must keep abreast of new procedures and treatments. They should be able to assume the responsibilities and duties of all citizens, cultivating their minds as they study and serve the society in which they live.

THE REWARDS

In the past, salaries of all workers in the health field were lower than salaries in business and industry for positions requiring a comparable amount of formal education and demanding as much responsibility. During those years, personnel directors had a favorite cliche. "This is the price you pay for the privilege of serving humanity."

Fortunately, those long years of low salaries never deterred or influenced anyone who wanted to become a physical therapist. Admittedly, the long hours of hard work, the great responsibility, and the low salaries did have a discouraging effect on many therapists whose college classmates were earning four times as much in business careers.

Recently, there have been dramatic changes in the salary scale and in the personal benefits for physical therapists. Today salaries compare favorably, and often exceed, with those for other positions demanding similar educational backgrounds and responsibility, such as teaching, library science, and social service.

Salaries alone, low or high, could never compensate a physical therapist for the physical expenditure of energy and the emotion spent on patients year in and year out. A mountain climber braves the hazards of a precipitous ascent in thin air because "the mountain is there." Mary McMillan, founder of the APTA, once said, "There was a job to be done, and I was there." The physical therapist invests his or her life in the patients because they, too, "are there." Patients are like magnets, drawing those who must devote their lives to the rehabilitation of the handicapped.

Physical therapy is more than a way of earning a living; it is a way of life. There is a story about a famous English architect, Sir Christopher Wren, that can be applied to physical therapy. Sir Christopher was inspecting the building of a cathedral that he had designed. He stopped to talk with the workers, and he asked three of them what they were doing. The first person answered, "Cutting a piece of stone." The second replied, "Earning five shillings a day." The third said, "Helping to build a cathedral." Like the third man, a physical therapist does not exercise a hip joint, or earn $50,000 a year, but helps people to rebuild lives.

WORKING CONDITIONS

In the United States, hospitals, institutions, and organizations that provide care for the sick and disabled usually provide pleasant working conditions. Most American hospitals have central heating during the winter and provide air conditioning in the summer. Some hospitals provide living quarters, meals, and laundry, either at cost or free, for their staffs.

Departments vary in size depending upon whether the department was designated as physical therapy before a new building was erected or whether it was stuck in the only space available in an aging and obsolete structure.

Space may be generous or limited; departments, crowded or spacious. In many institutions, physical therapy departments are located on a portion of a single floor. Sometimes, a department occupies several floors of an entire wing or, possibly, a whole building. Some departments have a number of generous-sized treatment and dressing rooms, exercise areas, and private offices. In other departments, there are curtained cubicles in one or two large rooms. Some departments must use corridors for gait training and waiting rooms, while others have luxurious furnishings. Some departments are light, airy, and quiet, while others are dark, stuffy, drafty, or noisy.

Therapists who treat patients in the patients' homes may find circumstances varying from servant-staffed mansions to rickety shacks in a poverty area, depending upon whether the service for home-bound patients is a private practice or a public health service. The therapist engaged in a home-bound service may spend a great deal of time traveling through summer heat or winter blizzards. At other times, however, the traveling therapist may pass through the fragrant apple blossoms of the spring and the breathtaking foliage of fall. Climate and weather must be taken into consideration.

Therapists who volunteer for foreign service will not always find working conditions pleasant and comfortable, but relatively few therapists work overseas.

The majority of employed therapists work forty hours a week. Traditionally, this has been Monday through Friday from 8:30 A.M. to 5:00 P.M. Some general hospitals are open on Saturday mornings, with rotation of a minimum staff. These persons are then given a half-day off during the week or are paid time-and-a-half for the overtime. Increasingly, departments are open on weekends. In some California institutions the departments are open twenty-four hours a day, seven days a week. With the recent health care budget cutbacks, and increasing demands by third-party payers for efficiency, physical therapists will probably treat patients in many hospitals seven days a week in the not too distant future.

Department directors who treat patients only 40 percent of the time are not eligible for overtime compensation, however, because they are grouped with administrative personnel.

The usual labor laws regarding luncheon and morning and afternoon breaks, legal holiday time, and vacation scheduling apply to physical therapists. Self-employed therapists do not have to observe the labor laws.

ADVANTAGES AND DISADVANTAGES

In a job, career, or profession, will you ever find a utopia? In any field there will be moments that are dull, routine, tedious, and irritating. No job can promise you a forty-hour workweek filled with constant mental stimulation, emotional reward, and recognition of your knowledge and ability. Every career has something special to offer you, and, simultaneously, every career lacks something you desire. You must exchange one thing for another. Only you can determine what you want to gain and what you prefer to reject.

Disadvantages exist in physical therapy just as in any other field. Specifically, the work is physically, mentally, and emotionally exhausting. You will be lifting patients who cannot move, and this is hard physical labor. The workload will be heavy because almost every department is inadequately staffed. Ironically, the shorter-staffed the department, the more urgent the need for additional recruits, but the more difficult it is to find replacements.

Despite the stress that physical therapists place on body mechanics, a sudden motion by a patient may catch a therapist off guard and cause an injury. Occasionally a therapist has been hospitalized in traction, braced, or operated on as a result of an injury suffered in the line of duty while performing routine tasks.

A day's work can leave you completely drained of energy because you are superimposing your will upon your patients' in an effort to draw from them the response you want. Often it is a response they don't want to make. You must achieve your result by positive encouragement, never by scolding and criticism. This is infinitely more fatiguing than the physical handling of patients.

The advantages of physical therapy as a career far outweigh the disadvantages. First, the job potential is constantly increasing. During the past few years, salaries have doubled and even tripled in some areas. Professions always offer prestige to those who practice them. Other health workers respect physical therapists for their role on the rehabilitation team. The lay public surrounds physical therapists with an aura of glamour because they help people walk again.

In actuality, the advantages and disadvantages are superficial. Physical therapy offers you an opportunity to participate in the drama of life. It gives you an opportunity to contribute to the world and not just to take from it.

If you need more information, contact APTA or visit their web site.

The American Physical Therapy Association
  1111 North Fairfax Street
  Alexandria, VA 22314-1488
  Phone: 703-684-2782
  http://www.apta.org/

CONCLUSION

President John F. Kennedy once said, "It is our task, in our time and in our generation, to hand down undiminished to those who come after us what was handed down to us by those who went before…to do this requires constant attention and vigilance, and sustained vigor and imagination."

Mary McMillan said much the same thing a bit differently; "Physical therapy isn't always easy. It's the hard knocks that bring out the best timber in us. Who wants a soft job anyway?"

ACCREDITED PROGRAMS

Alabama

University of Alabama at Birmingham
   Division of Physical Therapy
   School of Health Related Professions
   900 Nineteenth Street South
   Bishop Building, Room 102
   Birmingham, AL 35294-2030
   205-934-3566
   Fax: 205-975-7787

University of Mobile
   3 Mobile Infirmary Circle, Suite 308
   Mobile, AL 36607
   334-431-3941
   Fax: 334-431-3969

University of South Alabama
   Department of Physical Therapy
   1504 Spring Hill Avenue, Room 1214
   Mobile, AL 36604
   Admissions/Student Inquiries: 334-460-7962
   Fax: 334-434-3822

Arizona

Arizona School for Health Sciences, Kirksville College of
      Osteopathic Medicine
   Physical Therapy Program
   P.O. Box 11037
   Phoenix, AZ 85017
   602-841-4077
   Fax: 602-841-4092

Northern Arizona University
  Department of Physical Therapy
  CU Box 15105
  Flagstaff, AZ 86011
  520-523-4092
  Fax: 520-523-9289

Arkansas

Arkansas State University
  Physical Therapy Program
  College of Nursing and Health Professions
  P.O. Box 910
  State University, AR 72467-0910
  870-972-3591
  Admissions/Student Inquiries: 870-972-3591
  Financial Aid: 870-972-2310
  Fax: 870-972-2040

University of Central Arkansas
  Department of Physical Therapy
  201 Donaghey, PTC 100
  Conway, AR 72035-0001
  501-450-5548
  Admissions/Student Inquiries: 501-450-3611
  Financial Aid: 501-450-3140
  Fax: 501-450-5822

California

California State University, Fresno
  Physical Therapy Department
  2345 E. San Ramon Avenue
  MS-29
  Fresno, CA 93740-8031
  209-278-2022
  Fax: 209-278-3635

California State University, Long Beach
  Physical Therapy Department
  College of Health and Human Services
  1250 Bellflower Boulevard
  Long Beach, CA 90840
  562-985-4072
  Fax: 562-985-4069

California State University, Northridge
  Program in Physical Therapy
  Department of Health Sciences
  Northridge, CA 91330-8285
  818-677-3101
  Fax: 818-677-2045

California State University, Sacramento
  Degree Program in Physical Therapy
  School of Health and Human Services
  Sacramento, CA 95819-6020
  916-278-6426
  Admissions/Student Inquiries: 916-278-6426
  Financial Aid: 916-278-6554
  Fax: 916-278-5053

Chapman University
  School of Physical Therapy
  333 N. Glassell
  Orange, CA 92666
  714-744-7620
  Admissions/Student Inquiries: 714-997-6786
  Fax: 714-744-7621

Loma Linda University
  Department of Physical Therapy
  School of Allied Health Professions
  Loma Linda, CA 92350
  909-824-4632
  Fax: 909-824-4291

Mount St. Mary's College
  Department of Physical Therapy
  12001 Chalon Road
  Los Angeles, CA 90049
  310-954-4171
  Admissions/Student Inquiries: 310-954-4170
  Financial Aid: 310-954-4190
  Fax: 310-954-4179

Samuel Merritt College
  Department of Physical Therapy
  370 Hawthorne Avenue
  Oakland, CA 94609
  510-869-6241
  Admissions/Student Inquiries: 510-869-6576
  Financial Aid: 510-869-6131
  Fax: 510-869-6282

University of California, San Francisco/San Francisco State
    University
  UCSF/SFSU Graduate Program in Physical Therapy
  School of Medicine
  374 Parnassus, Box 0736
  San Francisco, CA 94143-0736
  415-338-2001 (SFSU)
  Fax: 415-338-0907

University of South California
  Department of Biokinesiology & Physical Therapy
  1540 E. Alcazar Street
  CHP 155
  Los Angeles, CA 90033
  323-442-2900
  Admissions/Students Inquiries: 323-442-2890
  Financial Aid: 323-442-2890
  Fax: 323-442-1515

University of the Pacific
  Department of Physical Therapy
  School of Pharmacy
  Stockton, CA 95211
  209-946-2886
  Admissions/Student Inquiries: 209-946-2886
  Financial Aid: 209-946-2421

Western University of Health Sciences
 Department of Physical Therapy Education
 352 Pomona Mall East
 Pomona, CA 91766-1854
 909-469-5294; 800-437-9474
 Admissions/Student Inquiries: 909-469-5338
 Financial Aid: 909-469-5355
 Fax: 909-629-7255

Colorado

Regis University
 Department of Physical Therapy
 3333 Regis Boulevard
 Denver, CO 80221-1099
 303-458-4340
 Financial Aid: 303-458-4066
 Fax: 303-964-5474

University of Colorado Health Science Center
 Physical Therapy Program
 4200 E. Ninth Avenue, Box C244
 Denver, CO 80262
 303-372-9144
 Fax: 303-372-9016

Connecticut

Quinnipiac College
 Program in Physical Therapy
 School of Health Sciences
 Mount Carmel Avenue
 Hamden, CT 06518
 203-281-5251
 Admissions/Student Inquiries: 203-281-8600
 Financial Aid: 203-281-8750
 Fax: 203-281-8706

University of Connecticut
   Department of Physical Therapy
   School of Allied Health Professions
   358 Mansfield Road, U-101
   Storrs, CT 06269-2101
   860-486-0049
   Admissions/Student Inquiries: 860-486-2834
   Financial Aid: 860-486-1588
   Fax: 860-486-1588

University of Hartford
   Physical Therapy Program
   Division of Health Professions
   200 Bloomfield Avenue
   West Hartford, CT 06117-1599
   860-768-5303
   Fax: 860-768-5244

Delaware

University of Delaware
   Department of Physical Therapy
   303 McKinly Laboratory
   Newark, DE 19716
   302-831-8910
   Fax: 302-831-4234

District of Columbia

Howard University
   Department of Physical Therapy
   College of Pharmacy, Nursing, and Allied Health Sciences
   Sixth and Bryant Streets NW
   Washington, DC 20059
   202-806-7613
   Fax: 202-806-7918

Florida

Florida Agricultural and Mechanical University
  Division of Physical Therapy
  School of Allied Health Sciences
  Room 223, Ware-Rhaney Building
  Tallahasee, FL 32307
  850-599-3820
  Fax: 850-561-2457

Florida International University
  Department of Physical Therapy
  College of Health Sciences
  Miami, FL 33199
  305-348-3831
  Fax: 305-348-1240

Nova Southeastern University
  Physical Therapy Program
  Health Profession Division
  College of Allied Health
  3200 S. University Drive
  Ft Lauderdale, FL 33328
  954-262-1662
  Fax: 954-262-1783

University of Central Florida
  Program in Physical Therapy
  4000 Central Florida Boulevard
  Trailer 544
  Orlando, FL 32816-2205
  407-823-3462
  Fax: 407-823-3464

University of Florida
  Department of Physical Therapy
  College of Health Professions
  Box 100154 HSC
  Gainesville, FL 32610-0154
  352-846-2379
  Fax: 352-392-6529

University of Miami
  Division of Physical Therapy
  Department of Orthopaedics & Rehabilitation
  School of Medicine
  5915 Ponce de Leon Boulevard, 5th Floor
  Coral Gables, FL 33146
  305-284-4535
  Fax: 305-284-6128

University of North Florida
  Physical Therapist Program
  College of Health
  4567 St. Johns Bluff Road South
  Jacksonville, FL 32224
  904-620-2840
  Fax: 904-620-2848

University of St. Augustine for Health Sciences
  Entry-level Master of Physical Therapy Program
  Institute of Physical Therapy
  1 University Boulevard
  St. Augustine, FL 32086
  904-826-0084
  Admissions/Student Inquiries: 904-826-0330
  Fax: 904-826-0085

Georgia

Armstrong Atlantic State University
  Department of Physical Therapy
  11935 Aberdeen Street
  Savannah, GA 31419-1997
  912-921-2327
  Fax: 912-921-5838

Emory University
  Division of Physical Therapy
  1441 Clifton Road, NE, Suite 423
  Atlanta, GA 30322
  404-712-5660
  Admissions/Student Inquiries: 404-712-5657
  Fax: 404-712-4130

Georgia State University
  Department of Physical Therapy
  University Plaza
  Atlanta, GA 30303
  404-651-3091
  Fax 404-651-1584

Medical College of Georgia
  Department of Physical Therapy
  School of Allied Health Sciences and Graduate Studies
  Augusta, GA 30912-0800
  706-721-2141
  Fax: 706-721-3209

North Georgia College and State University
  Graduate Program in Physical Therapy
  Barnes Hall, Room A-8
  Dahlonega, GA 30597
  706-864-1422
  Admissions/Student Inquiries: 706-864-1492
  Financial Aid: 706-864-1412
  Fax: 706-864-1493

Idaho

Idaho State University
  Department of Physical and Occupational Therapy
  College of Health Professions
  Box 8002
  Pocatello, ID 83209
  208-236-4095
  Fax: 208-236-4645

Illinois

Bradley University
  Department of Physical Therapy
  1501 W. Bradley Avenue
  Peoria, IL 61625
  309-677-3489
  Fax: 309-677-3445

Governors State University
  Physical Therapy Program
  College of Health Professions
  University Park, IL 60466
  708-534-7290
  Fax: 708-534-1647

Midwestern University
  Physical Therapy Program
  College of Allied Health Professions
  555 Thirty-First Street
  Downers Grove, IL 60515
  630-515-6462
  Admissions/Student Inquiries: 800-458-6253
  Fax: 630-515-7224

Northern Illinois University
  Physical Therapy Program
  School of Allied Health Professions
  DeKalb, IL 60115
  815-753-1383
  Admissions/Student Inquiries: 815-756-1383
  Financial Aid: 815-756-8236
  Fax: 815-753-0720

Northwestern University
  Programs in Physical Therapy
  The Medical School
  645 N. Michigan Avenue, Suite 1100
  Chicago, IL 60611-2814
  312-908-8160
  Admissions/Student Inquiries: 312-908-6786
  Fax: 312-908-0741

The Herman M. Finch University of Health Sciences/The Chicago
    Medical School
  Physical Therapy Department
  School of Related Health Sciences
  3333 Green Bay Road
  North Chicago, IL 60064
  847-578-3307
  Fax: 847-578-8816

The University of Illinois at Chicago
  Physical Therapy Education Program
  College of Associated Health Professions
  1919 W. Taylor, M/C 898
  Chicago, IL 60612
  312-996-7765
  Admissions/Student Inquiries: 312-996-4350
  Financial Aid: 312-996-3126
  Fax: 312-996-3807

Indiana

Indiana University
  Physical Therapy Program
  School of Allied Health Sciences
  1226 W. Michigan Street, Room 112
  Indianapolis, IN 46202-5180
  317-278-1875
  Fax: 317-278-1876

University of Evansville
  Department of Physical Therapy
  1800 Lincoln Avenue
  Evansville, IN 47722
  812-479-2345
  Admissions/Student Inquiries: 800-423-8633, ext. 2341
  Financial Aid: 812-479-2364
  Fax: 812-479-2717

University of Indianapolis
  Krannert School of Physical Therapy
  1400 E. Hanna Avenue
  Indianapolis, IN 46227-3697
  317-788-3500
  Fax: 317-788-3542

Iowa

Clarke College
  Department of Physical Therapy
  1550 Clarke Drive
  Dubuque, IA 52001-3198
  319-588-6382
  Admissions/Student Inquiries: 319-588-6316
  Financial Aid: 319-588-8153
  Fax: 319-588-6789

St. Ambrose University
  Physical Therapy Department
  College of Human Services
  518 W. Locust
  Davenport, IA 52803
  319-333-6403
  Admissions/Student Inquiries: 319-333-6403
  Financial Aid: 319-333-6314
  Fax: 319-333-6410

The University of Iowa
  Physical Therapy Graduate Program
  College of Medicine
  2600 Steindler Building
  Iowa City, IA 52242-1008
  319-335-9791
  Fax: 319-335-9707

University of Osteopathic Medicine & Health Sciences
  Program in Physical Therapy
  College of Health Sciences
  3200 Grand Avenue
  Des Moines, IA 50312
  515-271-1634
  Admissions/Student Inquiries: 800-240-2767
  Financial Aid: 515-271-1450
  Fax: 515-271-1714

Kansas

University of Kansas Medical Center
  Department of Physical Therapy Education
  3056 Robinson Hall
  3901 Rainbow Boulevard
  Kansas City, KS 66160-7601
  913-588-6799
  Fax: 913-588-4568

Wichita State University
  Department of Physical Therapy
  College of Health Professions
  1845 Fairmont
  Wichita, KS 67260-0043
  316-978-3604
  Fax: 316-978-3025

Kentucky

University of Kentucky
  Division of Physical Therapy
  213 CAHP Bldg.
  121 Washington Avenue
  Lexington, KY 40506-0003
  606-323-1100 ext. 258
  Fax: 606-257-1816

University of Louisville
  Program in Physical Therapy
  School of Allied Health Sciences
  K-Building
  Health Sciences Center
  Louisville, KY 40292
  502-852-7816
  Fax: 502-852-4597

Louisiana

Louisiana State University Medical Center
  Department of Physical Therapy
  School of Allied Health Professions
  1900 Gravier Street
  New Orleans, LA 70112
  504-568-4288
  Admissions/Student Inquiries: 504-568-4254
  Financial Aid: 504-568-4820
  Fax: 504-568-6552

Maine

University of New England
  Department of Physical Therapy
  11 Hills Beach Road
  Biddeford, ME 04005
  207-283-0171 ext. 2323
  Admissions/Student Inquiries: 207-283-0171, ext. 2297
  Financial Aid: 207-283-0171
  Fax: 207-283-4695

Maryland

University of Maryland—Baltimore
  Department of Physical Therapy
  School of Medicine
  100 Penn Street, Room 115
  Baltimore, MD 21201
  410-706-7720
  Financial Aid: 410-706-7776
  Fax: 410-706-6387

University of Maryland—Eastern Shore
  Department of Physical Therapy
  Kiah Hall, First Floor
  Princess Anne, MD 21853
  410-651-6360
  Fax: 410-651-6259

Massachusetts

American International College
  Physical Therapy Program
  1000 State Street
  Springfield, MA 01109-9983
  413-747-6412
  Admissions/Student Inquiries: 413-747-6201
  Financial Aid: 413-747-6259
  Fax: 413-788-9961

Boston University
  Department of Physical Therapy
  Sargent College of Health and Rehabilitation Sciences
  635 Commonwealth Avenue
  Boston, MA 02215
  617-353-2720
  Fax: 617-353-9463

MGH Institute of Health Professions
  Professional Program in Physical Therapy
  101 Merrimac Street
  Boston, MA 02114
  617-724-4841
  Admissions/Student Inquiries: 617-726-3140
  Fax: 617-726-4854

Northeastern University
  Department of Physical Therapy
  Room 6, Robinson Hall
  360 Huntington Avenue
  Boston, MA 02115
  617-373-3160
  Fax: 617-373-3161

Simmons College
  Graduate School for Health Studies
  Graduate Program in Physical Therapy
  300 The Fenway
  Boston, MA 02115
  617-521-2635
  Admissions/Student Inquiries: 617-521-2605
  Financial Aid: 617-521-2036
  Fax: 617-521-3137

Springfield College
  Department of Physical Therapy
  263 Alden St.
  Springfield, MA 01109
  413-748-3369
  Fax: 413-748-3371

University of Massachusetts, Lowell
  Program in Physical Therapy
  Weed Hall
  1 University Avenue
  Lowell, MA 01854-5095
  978-934-4517
  Admissions/Student Inquiries: 978-934-2380
  Financial Aid: 978-934-4220
  Fax: 978-934-3006

Michigan

Andrews University
  Department of Physical Therapy
  Berrien Springs, MI 49104-0420
  616-471-6551
  Admissions/Student Inquiries: 800-827-2878
  Fax: 616-471-2866

Central Michigan University
  Graduate Program in Physical Therapy
  134 Pearce Hall
  Mt. Pleasant, MI 48859
  517-774-2347
  Fax: 517-774-2908

Grand Valley State University
  Department of Physical Therapy
  328 Henry Hall
  Allendale, MI 49401
  616-895-3356
  Admissions/Student Inquiries: 616-895-3356
  Financial Aid: 616-895-3234
  Fax: 616-895-3350

Oakland University
  Program in Physical Therapy
  School of Health Sciences
  Rochester, MI 48309-4482
  248-370-4041
  Fax: 248-370-4287

University of Michigan—Flint
  Physical Therapy Department
  School of Health Professions and Studies
  Flint, MI 48502-2186
  810-762-3373
  Admissions/Student Inquiries: 810-762-3300
  Financial Aid: 810-762-3444
  Fax: 810-766-6668

Wayne State University
  Department of Physical Therapy
  439 Shapero Hall
  Detroit, MI 48202
  313-577-1432
  Fax: 313-577-5400

Minnesota

College of St. Catherine
  Physical Therapist Program
  601 Twenty-Fifth Avenue South
  Minneapolis, MN 55454
  612-690-7825
  Admissions/Student Inquiries: 612-690-6933
  Fax: 612-690-7849

College of St. Scholastica
  Department of Physical Therapy
  1200 Kenwood Avenue
  Duluth, MN 55811
  218-723-6786
  Admissions/Student Inquiries: 218-723-6285
  Financial Aid: 218-723-6397
  Fax: 218-723-6472

Mayo School of Health Related Sciences
  Physical Therapy Program
  Mayo Foundation
  200 First Street, SW
  Rochester, MN 55905
  507-284-2054
  Fax: 507-284-0656

University of Minnesota
    Program in Physical Therapy
    Box 388 UMHC
    Minneapolis, MN 55455
    612-626-5303
    Fax: 612-625-7192

Mississippi

University of Mississippi Medical Center
    Physical Therapy Department
    School of Health Related Professions
    2500 N. State Street
    Jackson, MS 39216-4505
    601-984-6330
    Fax: 601-984-6344

Missouri

Maryville University of St. Louis
    Department of Physical Therapy
    School of Health Care Professions
    13550 Conway Road
    St. Louis, MO 63141
    314-529-9523
    Fax: 314-529-9946

Rockhurst College
    Physical Therapy Education
    1100 Rockhurst Road
    Kansas City, MO 64110
    816-501-4059
    Admissions/Student Inquiries: 816-501-4174
    Financial Aid: 816-501-4100
    Fax: 816-501-4643

St. Louis University
    Department of Physical Therapy
    Health Sciences Center
    3437 Caroline Street, Room 1026
    St. Louis, MO 63104
    314-577-8505
    Fax: 314-577-8503

Southwest Baptist University
  Department of Physical Therapy
  1600 University Avenue
  Bolivar, MO 65613-2496
  417-326-1672
  Fax: 417-326-1658

University of Missouri-Columbia
  Department of Physical Therapy
  School of Health Related Professions
  106 Lewis Hall
  Columbia, MO 65211
  573-882-7103
  Fax: 573-884-8369

Washington University
  Program in Physical Therapy
  School of Medicine
  Campus Box 8502
  4444 Forest Park Boulevard, Suite 1101
  St. Louis, MO 63108
  314-286-1400
  Fax: 314-286-1410

Montana

University of Montana—Missoula
  Department of Physical Therapy
  Missoula, MT 59812
  406-243-4753
  Fax: 406-243-2795

Nebraska

Creighton University
  Physical Therapy Department
  School of Pharmacy and Allied Health Professions
  2500 California Plaza
  Omaha, NE 68178
  402-280-5675
  Fax: 402-280-5692

University of Nebraska Medical Center
  Division of Physical Therapy Education
  984420 Nebraska Medical Center
  Omaha, NE 68198-4420
  402-559-4259
  Financial Aid: 402-559-4199
  Fax: 402-559-8626

New Jersey

Rutgers, The State University of New Jersey, Graduate School,
    Camden/University of Medicine & Dentistry of New Jersey
  MPT Program
  Primary Care Center, Suite 228
  40 E. Laurel Road
  Stratford, NJ 08084-1353
  609-566-6456
  Admissions/Student Inquiries: 609-225-6104
  Financial Aid: 609-225-6039
  Fax: 609-566-6458

The Richard Stockton College of New Jersey
  Physical Therapy Program
  Jim Leeds Road
  Pomona, NJ 08240
  609-652-4261
  Admissions/Student Inquiries: 609-652-4261
  Financial Aid: 609-652-4261
  Fax: 609-652-4858

University of Medicine & Dentistry of New Jersey/Kean University/
    Seton Hall University
  Physical Therapy Program
  School of Health Related Professions
  65 Bergen Street
  Newark, NJ 07107-3001
  973-972-5454
  Fax: 973-972-3717

New Mexico

University of New Mexico
    Division of Physical Therapy
    Health Science and Service Building, Room 204
    Albuquerque, NM 87131-5661
    505-272-5755
    Fax: 505-272-8079

New York

Columbia University
    Program in Physical Therapy
    Columbia University
    710 W. 168th Street, 8th Floor
    New York, NY 10032
    212-305-3781
    Fax: 212-305-4569

D'Youville College
    Physical Therapy Program
    One D'Youville Square
    320 Porter Avenue
    Buffalo, NY 14201-1084
    716-881-7624
    Fax: 716-881-7790

Daemen College
    Physical Therapy Department
    4380 Main Street
    Amherst, NY 14226-3592
    716-839-8345
    Admissions/Student Inquiries: 716-839-8225
    Financial Aid: 716-839-8254
    Fax: 716-839-8516

Hunter College
    Physical Therapy Program
    School of Health Sciences
    425 E. Twenty-Fifth Street
    New York, NY 10010
    212-481-4469
    Admissions/Student Inquiries: 212-481-4320
    Fax: 212-481-4469

Ithaca College
  Department of Physical Therapy
  335 Smiddy Hall
  Ithaca, NY 14850-7183
  607-274-3342
  Admissions/Student Inquiries: 607-274-3124
  Financial Aid: 607-274-3131
  Fax: 607-274-1137

Long Island University—Brooklyn Campus
  Division of Physical Therapy
  Zeckendorf Health Sciences Center
  One University Plaza
  Brooklyn, NY 11201-5372
  718-488-1063 ext. 1501
  Admissions/Student Inquiries: 718-488-1011
  Fax: 718-780-4524

Mercy College
  Physical Therapy Program
  Graduate Center
  555 Broadway
  Dobbs Ferry, NY 10522
  914-674-9331 ext. 650
  Admission/Student Inquiries: 800-637-2969
  Fax: 914-674-9457

New York Medical College
  Program in Physical Therapy
  Graduate School of Health Sciences
  Learning Center, Room 302
  Valhalla, NY 10595
  914-594-4917
  Fax: 914-594-4292

New York University
  Department of Physical Therapy
  380 Second Avenue, 4th Floor
  New York, NY 10010-4086
  212-998-9400
  Fax: 212-995-4190

State University of New York at Buffalo
  Physical Therapy Program
  Department of Physical Therapy and Exercise and Nutrition
    Sciences
  405 Kimball Tower
  Buffalo, NY 14214-3079
  716-829-2941
  Fax: 716-829-2034

State University of New York at Stony Brook
  Department of Physical Therapy
  School of Health Technology and Management
  Health Sciences Center
  Stony Brook, NY 11794-8201
  516-444-3250
  Fax: 516-444-7621

State University of New York Health Science Center at Brooklyn
  Physical Therapy Program
  450 Clarkson Avenue, Box 16
  Brooklyn, NY 11203-2098
  718-270-7720
  Fax: 728-270-7439

State University of New York Health Science Center at Syracuse
  Department of Physical Therapy Education
  College of Health Professions
  750 E. Adams Street
  Syracuse, NY 13210
  315-464-5101
  Fax: 315-464-6914

The College of Staten Island
  Physical Therapy Program
  The City University of New York
  2800 Victory Boulevard
  Staten Island, NY 10314
  718-982-3153
  Fax: 718-982-2984

The Sage Colleges
Division of Health Rehabilitation Sciences Program
in Physical Therapy
Troy, NY 12180
518-244-2266
Fax: 518-270-2059

Touro College
Physical Therapy Program
Barry Z. Levine School of Allied Health Sciences
Building 10
135 Carman Road
Dix Hills, NY, 11746
516-673-3200, ext. 227
Admissions/Student Inquiries: 516-673-3200
Financial Aid: 516-673-3200
Fax: 516-673-3432

Utica College of Syracuse University
Department of Physical Therapy
Health and Human Studies Division
1600 Burrstone Road
Utica, NY 13502-4892
315-792-3006
Fax: 315-792-3248

North Carolina

Duke University
Graduate Program in Physical Therapy
P.O. Box 3965
Durham, NC 27710
919-684-2445 ext. 2650

East Carolina University
Department of Physical Therapy
School of Allied Health Sciences
Greenville, NC 27858-4353
919-328-4450
Fax: 919-328-0707

The University of North Carolina at Chapel Hill
  Division of Physical Therapy
  Medical School Wing E
  CB #7135
  Chapel Hill, NC 27599-7135
  919-966-4708
  Fax: 919-966-3678

Western Carolina University
  Department of Physical Therapy
  Cullowhee, NC 28723-9646
  828-227-7070
  Fax: 828-227-7071

Winston-Salem State University
  Physical Therapy Program
  601 Martin Luther King Jr. Drive
  Winston-Salem, NC 27110
  336-750-2190
  Fax: 336-750-2192

North Dakota

University of Mary
  Program in Physical Therapy
  7500 University Drive
  Bismarck, ND 58504-9652
  701-255-7500
  Fax: 701-255-7687

University of North Dakota
  Department of Physical Therapy
  School of Medicine
  P.O. Box 9037
  501 N. Columbia Road
  Grand Forks, ND 58202-9037
  701-777-2831
  Fax: 701-777-4199

Ohio

Andrew University/Dayton
  Department of Physical Therapy
  2912 Springboro West, Suite 301
  Dayton, OH 45439
  937-298-2878
  Admissions/Student Inquiries: 800-827-2878
  Financial Aid: 616-471-3334
  Fax: 937-298-9500

Cleveland State University
  Physical Therapy Program
  Department of Health Sciences
  1983 E. Twenty-Fourth Street
  Fenn Tower 609
  Cleveland, OH 44115
  216-687-3567
  Admissions/Student Inquiries: 216-687-3566
  Financial Aid: 216-687-3764
  Fax: 216-687-9316

Medical College of Ohio in Consortium with: Bowling Green State
    University and The University of Toledo
  Department of Physical Therapy
  4418 Collier Building
  3015 Arlington Avenue
  Toledo, OH 43614
  419-383-3518
  Fax: 419-383-5880

Ohio University
  School of Physical Therapy
  Room 172, Convocation Center
  Athens, OH 45701
  740-593-1225
  Fax: 740-593-0292

The Ohio State University
  Physical Therapy Division
  306 Allied Medical Professions
  1583 Perry Street
  Columbus, OH 43210
  614-292-5921
  Fax: 614-292-0210

The University of Findlay
  Physical Therapist Program
  1000 N. Main Street
  Findlay, OH 45840
  419-424-4863
  Admissions/Student Inquiries: 419-424-4863
  Financial Aid: 419-424-4792
  Fax: 419-424-6977

University of Cincinnati
  Physical Therapy Program
  College of Allied Health Sciences
  P.O. Box 210168
  Cincinnati, OH 45221-0168
  513-558-3351
  Fax: 513-556-4560

Youngstown State University
  Department of Physical Therapy
  One University Plaza
  Youngstown, OH 44555-2558
  330-742-2558
  Fax: 330-742-1898

Oklahoma

Langston University
  Physical Therapy Program
  School of Nursing and Health Professions
  P.O. Box 1500
  Langston, OK 73050
  405-466-3411
  Fax: 405-466-2915

University of Oklahoma Health Sciences Center
Department of Physical Therapy
P.O. Box 26901
College of Allied Health, Room 235
Oklahoma City, OK 73190
405-271-2131
Fax: 405-271-2432

Oregon

Pacific University
School of Physical Therapy
2043 College Way
Forest Grove, OR 97116
503-359-2846
Fax: 503-359-2995

Pennsylvania

Beaver College
Department of Physical Therapy
450 S. Easton Road
Glenside, PA 19038-3295
215-572-2950
Fax: 215-572-2157

Chatham College
Physical Therapy Program
Woodland Road
Pittsburgh, PA 15232-2826
412-365-1409
Admissions/Student Inquiries: 412-365-1292
Financial Aid: 800-837-1290
Fax: 412-365-1213

College Misericordia
Physical Therapy Department
Division of Health Sciences
301 Lake Street
Dallas, PA 18612-1098
570-674-6465
Admissions/Student Inquiries: 570-675-4449
Financial Aid: 570-674-6280
Fax: 570-674-8902

Duquesne University
  Department of Physical Therapy
  John G. Rangos Sr. School of Health Sciences
  111 Health Sciences Building
  Pittsburgh, PA 15282
  412-396-5541
  Fax: 412-396-4399

Gannon University
  Physical Therapy Program
  College of Sciences, Engineering, & Health Sciences
  AJ Palumbo Academic Center
  109 University Square
  Erie, PA 16541-0001
  814-871-5639
  Fax: 814-871-5662

MCP Hahnemann University
  Entry-level Master's Degree Program in Physical Therapy
  MS 502
  Broad and Vine
  Philadelphia, PA 19102
  215-762-1751
  Admissions/Student Inquiries: 215-762-4974
  Financial Aid: 215-762-7739
  Fax: 215-762-3886

Neumann College
  Physical Therapy Program
  Division of Nursing and Health Sciences
  One Neumann Drive
  Aston, PA 19014-1298
  610-558-5534
  Fax: 610-459-1370

Slippery Rock University of Pennsylvania
 Graduate School of Physical Therapy
 Suite 100, North Road
 Slippery Rock, PA 16057
 724-738-2080
 Fax: 724-738-2113

Temple University
 Department of Physical Therapy
 College of Allied Health Professions
 3307 N. Broad Street
 Philadelphia, PA 19140
 215-707-4815
 Fax: 215-707-7500

Thomas Jefferson University
 Department of Physical Therapy
 College of Health Professions
 130 S. Ninth Street
 Suite 830 Edison
 Philadelphia, PA 19107-5233
 215-503-8025
 Admissions/Student Inquiries: 215-503-1040
 Financial Aid: 215-955-2867
 Fax: 215-503-3499

University of Pittsburgh
 Department of Physical Therapy
 School of Health and Rehabilitation Sciences
 6035 Forbes Tower
 Pittsburgh, PA 15260
 412-647-1252
 Fax: 412-647-1222

University of Scranton
  Department of Physical Therapy
  800 Linden Street
  Scranton, PA 18510-4586
  717-941-7494
  Fax: 717-941-7940

University of the Sciences, in Philadelphia
  Physical Therapy Program
  600 S. Forty-Third Street
  Philadelphia, PA 19104
  215-596-8849
  Admissions/Student Inquiries: 215-596-8810
  Fax: 215-895-3121

Widener University
  Physical Therapy Program
  School of Human Service Professions
  One University Place
  Chester, PA 19013
  610-499-1277
  Fax: 610-499-1231

Puerto Rico

University of Puerto Rico–Medical Sciences Campus
  Physical Therapy Program, Undergraduate Department
  College of Health Related Professions
  P.O. Box 365067
  San Juan, PR 00936-5067
  787-758-2525
  Fax: 787-759-3645

Rhode Island

University of Rhode Island
Physical Therapy Program
Independence Square II
25 West Independence Way
Kingston, RI 02881-0180
401-874-5001
Fax: 401-874-5630

South Carolina

Medical University of South Carolina
Physical Therapy Education Program
Department of Rehabilitation Sciences
171 Ashley Avenue
Charleston, SC 29425-2730
803-792-2961
Fax: 803-792-0710

South Dakota
University of South Dakota
Department of Physical Therapy
414 E. Clark
Vermillion, SD 57069
605-677-5915
Fax: 605-677-6529

Tennessee

East Tennessee State University
Department of Physical Therapy
Box 70624
Johnson City, TN 37614-0624
423-439-7197
Admissions/Student Inquiries: 423-439-8275
Financial Aid: 423-439-4300
Fax: 423-439-8305

Tennessee State University
  Physical Therapy Department
  3500 John A. Merritt Boulevard
  Box 9564
  Nashville, TN 37209-1561
  615-963-5881
  Fax: 615-963-5935

The University of Tennessee at Chattanooga
  Department of Physical Therapy
  School of Rehabilitation Professions
  302 Health and Human Services Building
  615 McCallie Avenue
  Chattanooga, TN 37403-2598
  423-755-4747
  Fax: 423-785-2215

The University of Tennessee, Memphis
  Department of Physical Therapy
  822 Beale Street, Suite 337
  Memphis, TN 38163
  901-448-5888
  Fax: 901-448-7545

Texas

Hardin-Simmons University
  Department of Physical Therapy
  2200 Hickory
  Box 16065
  Abilene, TX 79698-6065
  915-670-5860
  Admissions/Student Inquiries: 888-820-0218
  Financial Aid: 915-670-1331
  Fax: 915-670-5868

Southwest Texas State University
  Department of Physical Therapy
  Health Science Center
  601 University Drive
  San Marcos, TX 78666-4616
  512-245-8351
  Financial Aid: 512-245-2315
  Fax: 512-245-8736

Texas Tech University Health Sciences Center
  Program in Physical Therapy
  3601 Fourth Street
  Lubbock, TX 79430
  806-743-3220
  Fax: 806-743-1262

Texas Woman's University
  School of Physical Therapy
  P.O. Box 425766, TWU Station
  Denton, TX 76204-5766
  940-898-2460
  Admissions/Student Inquiries: 940-898-2460
  Fax: 940-898-2486

The University of Texas Health Science Center at San Antonio
  Department of Physical Therapy
  7703 Floyd Curl Drive
  San Antonio, TX 78284-7781
  210-567-3150
  Fax: 210-567-3156

The University of Texas Medical Branch at Galveston
  Department of Physical Therapy
  School of Allied Health Sciences
  301 University Boulevard
  Galveston, TX 77555-1028
  409-772-3068
  Admissions/Student Inquiries: 409-772-3068
  Financial Aid: 409-772-4955
  Fax: 409-747-1613

University of Texas at El Paso
  Physical Therapy Program
  College of Nursing and Health Sciences
  1101 North Campbell
  El Paso, TX 79902-0581
  915-747-8207
  Admissions/Student Inquiries: 915-747-8207
  Financial Aid: 915-747-5204
  Fax: 915-747-8211

University of Texas Southwestern Medical Center at Dallas
  Department of Physical Therapy
  Southwestern Allied Health Sciences School
  5323 Harry Hines Boulevard
  Dallas, TX 75235-8876
  214-648-1551
  Admissions/Student Inquiries: 214-648-1550
  Financial Aid: 214-648-3611
  Fax: 214-648-1511

U.S. Army-Baylor University
  Graduate Program in Physical Therapy
  Academy of Health Sciences
  MCCS-HMT, Physical Therapy Branch
  3151 Scott Road
  Ft. Sam Houston, TX 78234-6138
  210-221-8410
  Fax: 210-221-7585

Utah

University of Utah
  Division of Physical Therapy
  College of Health
  Annex 1130, Wing B
  Salt Lake City, UT 84112
  801-581-8681
  Fax: 801-585-5629

Vermont

University of Vermont
  Department of Physical Therapy
  School of Allied Health Sciences
  305 Rowell Building
  Burlington, VT 05405-0068
  802-656-3252
  Fax: 802-656-2191

Virginia

Old Dominion University
  Program in Physical Therapy
  School of Community Health Professions and Physical Therapy
  Health Science Building
  Norfolk, VA 23529-0288
  757-683-4519
  Fax: 757-683-4410

Shenandoah University
  Program in Physical Therapy
  School of Health Professions
  333 W. Cork Street
  Winchester, VA 22601
  540-665-5520
  Admissions/Student Inquiries: 800-432-2266
  Financial Aid: 540-665-4538
  Fax: 540-665-5530

Virginia Commonwealth University
  Department of Physical Therapy
  Box 980224
  Medical College of Virginia Campus
  Richmond, VA 23298-0224
  804-828-0234
  Fax: 804-828-8111

Washington

Eastern Washington University
  Department of Physical Therapy
  526 Fifth Street, MS 4
  Cheney, WA 99004-2431
  509-623-4277
  Fax: 509-623-4321

University of Puget Sound
  School of Physical Therapy
  1500 N. Warner
  Tacoma, WA 98416
  253-756-3281
  Admissions/Student Inquiries: 253-756-3211
  Financial Aid: 253-756-3214
  Fax: 253-756-8309

University of Washington
  Division of Physical Therapy, CC-902
  Department of Rehabilitation Medicine
  1959 NE Pacific Street
  Box 356490
  Seattle, WA 98195-6490
  206-685-7408
  Fax: 206-685-3244

West Virginia

West Virginia University
  Division of Physical Therapy
  Department of Human Performance and Applied Exercise Science
  School of Medicine
  P.O. Box 9226
  Morgantown, WV 26506-9226
  304-293-3610
  Admissions/Student Inquiries: 304-293-3611
  Fax: 304-293-7105

Wheeling Jesuit University
  Physical Therapy Department
  316 Washington Avenue
  Wheeling, WV 26003
  304-243-2359
  Fax: 304-243-2042

Wisconsin

Carroll College
  Department of Physical Therapy
  100 North East Avenue
  Waukesha, WI 53186
  800-227-7650
  Fax: 414-524-7690

Concordia University Wisconsin
  Division of Physical Therapy
  12800 N. Lake Shore Drive
  Mequon, WI 53092-7699
  414-243-4433
  Admissions/Student Inquiries: 414-243-4300
  Financial Aid: 414-243-4348
  Fax: 414-243-4506

Marquette University
  Department of Physical Therapy
  P.O. Box 1881
  Milwaukee, WI 53201-1881
  414-288-7149
  Admissions/Student Inquiries: 414-288-7302
  Financial Aid: 414-288-7390
  Fax: 414-288-5987

University of Wisconsin—LaCrosse
  Department of Physical Therapy
  2032 Cowley Hall
  LaCrosse, WI 54601
  608-785-8470
  Fax: 608-785-8460

University of Wisconsin-Madison
  Physical Therapy Program
  5175 Medical Sciences Center
  1300 University Avenue
  Madison, WI 53706-1532
  608-263-7131
  Admissions/Student Inquiries: 608-265-4815
  Financial Aid: 608-262-3060
  Fax: 608-263-6434

Canada

Dalhousie University
  School of Physiotherapy
  5869 University Avenue
  Halifax, Nova Scotia
  CANADA B3H 3J5
  902-494-2524
  Fax: 902-494-1941

McGill University
  Physical Therapy Program
  3654 Drummond Street
  Montreal, Quebec
  CANADA H3G 1Y5
  514-398-4500
  Fax: 514-398-6360

McMaster University
  Physiotherapy Program
  School of Rehabilitation Science
  Building T-16
  1280 Main Street, W
  Hamilton, Ontario
  CANADA L8N 3Z5
  905-525-9140
  Fax: 905-524-0069

Queen's University
  Division in Physical Therapy
  School of Rehabilitation Therapy
  Faculty of Health Sciences
  Kingston, Ontario
  CANADA K7L 3N6
  613-545-6103
  Fax: 613-545-6776

Universite de Montreal
  (This program is offered in French.)
  Programme de Physiotherapie
  Ecole de readaptation
  CP 6128—Succursale Centre-ville
  Montreal, Quebec
  CANADA H3C 3J7
  514-343-7833
  Fax: 514-343-2105

Universite Laval
  (This program is given in French.)
  Physiotherapy Department
  Faculty of Medicine
  Pavillon Vandry
  Quebec City, Quebec
  CANADA G1K 7P4
  418-656-2874
  Fax: 418-656-5476

University of Alberta
  Department of Physical Therapy
  Faculty of Rehabilitation Medicine
  Room 2-50 Corbett Hall
  Edmonton, Alberta
  CANADA T6G 2G4
  403-492-5949
  Admissions/Student Inquiries: 403-492-5949
  Fax: 403-492-1626

University of British Columbia
  Division of Physical Therapy
  School of Rehabilitation Sciences
  T325-Third Floor-Koerner Pavillion
  2211 Wesbrook Mall
  Vancouver, British Columbia
  CANADA V6T 2B5
  604-822-7392
  Fax: 604-822-7624

University of Manitoba
  Division of Physical Therapy
  School of Medical Rehabilitation
  Faculty of Medicine
  770 Bannatyne Avenue
  Winnipeg, Manitoba
  CANADA R3E 0W3
  Admissions/Student Inquiries: 204-789-3674
  Financial Aid: 204-474-9531
  204-789-3897
  Fax: 204-789-3927

University of Saskatchewan
  School of Physical Therapy
  1121 College Drive
  Saskatoon, Saskatchewan
  CANADA S7N 0W3
  306-966-6579
  Fax: 306-966-6575

University of Western Ontario
  School of Physical Therapy
  Faculty of Health Sciences
  Elborn College
  London, Ontario
  CANADA N6G 1H1
  519-661-3360
  Fax: 519-661-3866

France

Centre Europeen d'Enseignement en Reeducation et Readaptation
    Fonctionel
  (This program is offered in French.)
  Physical Therapy Program
  7 Rue Danielle Cassanova
  93200 Saint Denis
  FRANCE
  011-331-30 30 10 36
  U.S. Inquiries: 404-229-3963
  Admissions/Student Inquiries: 404-229-3963
  Fax: 011-331-30 30 38 15

The Netherlands

Fontys Hogescholen Eindhoven
  (This course is given in English and Dutch.)
  Department of Physiotherapy
  Faculty Gamma
  Postbus 347
  5600 AH Eindhoven
  THE NETHERLANDS
  011-31-040-260-5768
  Fax: 011-31-40-246-5869

University of Professional Education Hogeschool Enschede
  (This program is offered in Dutch and has a four-year expansion
    program offered in English.)
  Department of Physical Therapy
  Postbus 70.000
  7500 KB Enschede
  THE NETHERLANDS
  011-31-53-4871521
  Fax: 011-31-53-4320373